Image and Meaning:

Metaphoric Traditions in Renaissance Poetry

DON CAMERON ALLEN

Image and Meaning

Metaphoric Traditions

in

Renaissance Poetry

Baltimore: The Johns Hopkins Press

Printed in the United States of America by
Vail-Ballou Press, Inc., Binghamton, N.Y.
Library of Congress Catalog Card Number 60–11408

This book has been brought to publication with
the assistance of a grant from The Ford Foundation.

Contents

Introduction

The essays in this book are experiments in reading learned poems. Most of them have been publicly read before, and I return to them not out of dissatisfaction but only to offer readings made in a different way. There are probably many ways to read a poem; there is certainly not one way. I like to read poetry when it is possible in terms of its poetical antecedents. This method does not permit me to explain how the poet wrote the poem or how a contemporary of the poet read it. I once thought it possible to approximate one or the other of these critical ends. Now I am convinced that it is impossible to read a poem as a contemporary of the poet might have read it. One can explain lost references, one can annotate the poem from the historical remnants of its generation, but this is not giving it a contemporary reading. If we were told, "Let us read this poem as a contemporary," we might ask which contemporary the speaker has in mind. Since I cannot come close to reading an Elizabethan poem as an Elizabethan would, I can hardly have the bad taste to argue that I know how Spenser, Shakespeare, or Marvell wrote a poem. This volume is, then, a poor attempt of a modern who has read earlier poetry to read a later poem.

In general I have tried to use only poetical annotations in my commentary. Since my material is poems, I have not pushed them into another language. I have tried to suggest what they mean with a summary or a rendering of the necessary metaphor. I have not been so pedantic about the non-literary texts which I have translated because I could do them no harm.

I am grateful to the editors of *Comparative Literature* and *Studies in Philology* for permission to reprint the two essays on Spenser and to the editor of the *Modern Language Quarterly* for the right to use the Lovelace essay. I am equally grateful to the editors of The Johns Hopkins Press for their patience with my vagaries and eccentricities. The Macmillan Company has kindly permitted me to quote the passage at the end of the Vaughan explication from John Masefield, *Collected Poems*, New York, 1935.

I must thank the American Council of Learned Societies for a grant which enabled me to put aside my pedagogical and administrative duties for a semester and visit a few libraries in search of useful books. This is the fifth book that that organization's bounty has enabled me to put together, and I should like to acknowledge its continuing help to me.

Baltimore, 1959   D. C. A.

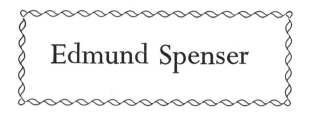

CHAPTER ONE

Edmund Spenser

"The March Eclogue" of
The Shepheardes Calender

"The March Eclogue" of *The Shepheardes Calender* is the attempt of a young poet to understand the nature of love. The force of the passion, that expresses itself in smiles and snarls, that is weak when it should be strong, strong when it should be mild, was as yet hardly known to him. He had just reached maturity when he wrote this poem, but he already sensed, as Thomalin (the main character of this eclogue) does, the painful joy and the joyful pain of love. Thanks to poets who had spoken about these matters before, the youthful Spenser was able to talk maturely while he still felt only the first warm flashes of a life that had more passion and pain than he had ever imagined. The problem that he discusses in this eclogue is not a new one and to understand what he has to say we may listen first to Bion, who discourses on a similar theme in his poem about the young birdcatcher.

A bird-catcher yet a boy in a woody grove
Was hunting birds when he saw winged Eros
Perched on the young shoot of a box tree. When he saw it,
He rejoiced because to him it seemed a big bird.
At once he bound his reeds together, one on another,
To catch Eros, who kept hopping here and there and fled
                                                      him.
And the boy, being vexed that his task was endless,
Threw down his reeds and went to an old farmer
Who taught him the art, and told it to him,
And showed him Eros perching; but the old man,
Smiling, shook his head and spoke to the boy:
"Refrain from this hunting and stay away from this bird!
Fly far! This is a bad bird! You will be happy
As long as you do not catch him. But when you have man's
                                                   measure,
This thing which now flees and hops away of its own
                                                    accord
Will come suddenly and sit on your head."

Even when the graceful Greek of Bion is turned into a
dull, literal English translation, we have no difficulty in identifying this bird. He is the runaway Eros of Moschus,[1] still
fugitive, yet the mysterious center of Bion's idyll. In Moschus'
poem, his Cyprian mother describes him for lovers so that
"he might be known among twenty others"; but Bion never
gives him proportion because he sees him only with the eyes
of a boy on the edge of adolescence, a visual and psychological
station that is established by the opening phrase of the poem.
But the boy birdcatcher, who represents the anticipatory aspects of life as opposed to the old husbandman who has, to
use the Greek expression, "turned the page of love," is not
completely without experience. He has gone into the world
(the grove filled with trees) to hunt birds (symbols of mature
activities), carrying with him the engines necessary to man-

[1] *Eidyllion* I.

hood but for the moment inadequate for what he encounters. The boy of the idyll has speculated, perhaps, on the grown-up occupation with love; it has come before his eyes, but as yet he cannot understand it. It is, consequently, like a bird, singing and fluttering, but masked in its true and curious nature by the dense foliage of the wood of life.

To underscore the insufficiency of the boy's knowledge, Bion says that Eros lights on a "young shoot" of the box tree, and adds that to the boy it is a "big bird." This childlike descriptive phrase is attended by a childlike verb, for the boy "rejoices" at the sight. These are sophisticated attempts to reproduce an adolescent's verbal reactions to what he half perceives. The verb φαίνετο, which controls the fourth line of the poem, suggests the external; the boy sees only the bare outline of Eros. Because a Greek boy often sought the advice of his teachers, this young hunter turns quickly to the old man from whom he had learned his art. This youthful decision further demonstrates the boy's unworldliness.

The *senex* sees the "big bird" and ungraciously translates it into "κακόν . . . θηρίον" (wicked beast); in fact, when he uses the proper generic word, he distinguishes it with "τόδε" (*this* bird). He speaks at once; the bird must be avoided, not hunted. The old husbandman undoubtedly knows all that the Aphrodite of Moschus had said about her son. "If you catch him, he will lead you captive. He will betray you by weeping. His lips are poison." All of this the rural adviser, unwilling to state the alluring particulars, puts into blunt precept. More subtly, and perhaps sadly, he says that the time may arrive when Love, who now eludes him, will come of his own accord, a probability that the ambiguous "τὸν ἀπότροπον . . . Ἔρωτα" of the second line suggests. Love, "flying and to be fled," says the old man, will settle itself, not on the young shoot of the boxtree, but on *your* head.

The ploughman of the Greek idyll is a forbidding *magister*

amoris; he has taught the youth his arts, but he gives him no
real advice on the "τέχνη ἐρωτική." We must look to the Roman
elegiac poets, to Tibullus or Propertius, repeaters of the tropes
of Callimachus, or to Ovid, to find the full detail that illumi-
nates the taciturnity of Bion's old man. These poets tell us how
love is hunted with tears and wounds. Once it is caught, its
plumage is found to be as false as its eyes and heart. Fortunately, this sour attitude is not the only one because, when
Bion's poem is held up to the light, we see between its lines
another old teacher who is kinder and more joyous.

Three hundred years after the death of Bion, the *fabula*
of his delicate poem was repeated when Philetas, a rural Orpheus, told the story of Eros to the young lovers, Daphnis
and Chloe. It is the story of the old shepherd's experience, not
in the wood, but in a pleasant garden that he had made with
his hands.

> As I went in there today about noon, a boy appeared in the
> pomegranate and myrtle grove . . . [he was] white as milk and
> his hair shining with the glance of fire. . . . Naked he was,
> alone he was; he played and wantoned it about, and culled and
> pulled as if it were his garden. Therefore, I ran at him as fast
> as I could, thinking to get him in my clutches. . . . But he, with
> a soft and easy sleight, gave me the slip, sometimes running
> under the roses, sometimes hiding himself in the poppies.[2]

The little god, who is still Bion's elusive bird, refuses to be
questioned, but eventually he speaks with the voice of a wood
thrush to the old lover. "I may not be taken," he says, "though
a hawk or an eagle or any other swifter bird be flown at me,
I am not a boy though I seem to be one, but am older than
Saturn and all this universe." He informs Philetas that it was
he who managed that Philetas and his beloved wife Amaryllis
meet: "I was at her side, but you did not see me." Then he
adds, "Be glad, Philetas, that you alone of all mortals have

[2] Longus II.3–8.

seen this boy in your old age." Having said this, the boy Eros
skips from bough to bough like a nightingale, and the question
of Daphnis and Chloe about the nature of Eros, boy or bird,
is almost answered. The young couple never see the god although they are in his province; and the truth that emerges
and that seems to color Spenser's March eclogue is that Eros,
the feathered thing, manifests himself only to those who stand
on the threshold of maturity or to those others who have
passed out of love's limits and look back on its sunny counties
through the defiles of memory.

For the old shepherd Philetas, the recollection of love is
good, and he is truly a *magister amoris maximus* like Tibullus [3]
or Ovid.[4] It is, therefore, not without point that Eros describes
the flowers in the old man's garden as "poems," "τὰ φυτὰ ταυτα
τούτου ποιήματα." [5] The old husbandman in Bion's poem has, on
the other hand, shabby memories, which are shared by the old
woman who takes his place when Ronsard brings the whole
topic into French poetry. The old gentleman on whom both
the *presbyter* and the *saga* are fashioned is probably hoary
Cephalus, whom Socrates, no youth but an habitual bearer of
limed twigs, once consulted about the nature of passionate
love. "Never," said that old man, "lament the passing of love,
but say with Sophocles: 'Hush, to my great delight I have escaped it and feel free of a despot who was desperate and
angry.' " [6] It is this mood, rather than the playful one of Bion
or the happy one of Longus, that drifts like a cold mist
through Ronsard's poem.

The transition from Bion's sensitively conceived contrast

---

[3] "Vos me celebrate magistrum,/Quos male habet multa callidus arte
puer./Gloria cuique sua est: me, qui spernentur, amantes/ Consultent; cunc-
tis ianua nostra patet./ Tempus erit, cum me Veneris praecepta ferentem/
Deducat iuvenum sedula turba senem" (I.iv.75–80).
[4] "Inscribit spoliis, Naso magister erat" (*Ars* II.744).
[5] II.7.
[6] *Republic* I.329C.

between the attitudes of extreme youth and age in the revealed presence of the great god Eros to Ronsard's bitter
modification of the theme [7] can be made in part on the topic
of the *magister amoris*, who joins with the witch of the Latin
poets to make a new person for the gardens of love. The boy
in Ronsard's poem has been trying to catch birds for his cage
when suddenly he sees Eros "comme oyseau de mauvais
augure."

> Un enfant dedans un bocage
> Tendoit finement ses gluaux,
> A fin de prendre des oyseaux
> Pour les emprisonner en cage.
>   Quand il veit, par cas d'adventure,
> Pres un buys Amour emplumé
> Qui voloit par le boys ramé
> Comme oyseau de mauvais augure.

The "big bird" and the naïveté of the Greek poem are gone,
and, by direct intent, love is polluted with ill qualities; for the
winged God of Love has now become "l'oyseau de mauvaise
rencontre." On further inspection, the "enfant" discovers the
peacock colors of the bird's wings and that "sa face sembloit
un Ange/ Qu'on voit portrait en un tableau." This comparison
of Eros and an angel bothers us only until we remember that
Cupid was for some men of the Middle Ages a fallen angel.
Ronsard's "enfant" partly reproduces the experience of Bion's
boy; he also "rejoices" but it is in the hope of snaring "si grand
proye." The bird will not be surprised; and so in rage, the boy
drops his lures and

> Vint trouver une vielle mere
> Qui se mesloit de deviner.

[7] I follow Laumonier's 1934 text, VII.259–62. The description of Eros in
this poem comes from Moschus, I, via Poliziano's Latin rendering and
Baif's French version.

The *magistri* step aside so that Phryne, the witch who can fetch and dismiss love, may enter from another tradition. It is clear that Ronsard's "mere" is not an old teacher of the boy; she is also no happy Amaryllis. She is gray-haired and sour-faced and as disillusioned with love as she is with life. She is Medea at sixty, and in literature she has many cousins. Propertius tells us that she is both instructress in the affairs of the heart and mistress of magic arts.[8] She is the witch of Atlas whom Dido remembered so well;[9] but she is best known to us through a poem by Tibullus, a poem that ends like a sorceress' incantation.

> Hanc ego de caelo ducentem sidera vidi;
>   Fluminis haec rapidi carmine vertit iter,
> Haec cantu finditque solum manesque sepulchris
>   Elicit et tepido devocat ossa rogo;
> Iam tenet infernas magico stridore catervas,
>   Iam iubet aspersas lacte referre pedem.
> Cum libet, haec tristi depellit nubila caelo:
>   Cum libet, aestivo convocat orbe nives,
> Sola tenere malas Medeae dicitur herbas,
>   Sola feros Hecatae perdomuisse canes.[10]

The "vielle mere" is a *verax saga amoris*, and Ronsard certainly thought, as he wrote, of her haunting song expressed by his beloved Theocritus:

φράζεό μευ τὸν ἔρωθ' ὅθεν ἵκετο, πότνα Σελάνα [11]

This woman whom Ronsard displays in her dour and bitter years was once one of those lively young witches, a Simaetha who could beguile men's hearts, as Propertius [12] tells us, by charming the moon from the heavens. Now she has reached

---

[8] IV.5.
[9] *Aeneid* IV.478–91.
[10] I.ii.43–52.
[11] II.81.
[12] I.i.19–20.

the time in life when all seems stale. She is La Vielle of the
Roman de la Rose, Dame Brysenne of the *Mort d'Arthur*, or,
on a lower social level, Villon's Belle Heaulmière. Regnier
writes about her in the seventeenth century; [13] and we shall
see her again in Ronsard's "Contra Denise Sorciere," a poem
that is founded on Horace's assault against Canidia and that
shines with antique spoils. In all instances, she is a gray woman
who scorns her recollections of love, and, like her predecessor
in Bion, is a kind of Anteros, the half-brother of Eros, who
saw to it in ancient times that love was reciprocated, but who
had come to stand for his opponent, a violent Anti-Eros. [14]
In both her person and her advice, the "mere" consulted by
Ronsard's "garcon" is a personification of the enemies of Cupid. At one time she may have provided her clients with
philtres to bring love, but she no longer practises fascination.
Her charms and spells now effect the contrary.

Toward the center of her homily, she says to the youth:

> O que tu seras bien heureux
> Si tu le fuys toute ta vie
> Et si jamais tu n'as envye
> D'estre au rolle des amoreux.

"Stay off the register of lovers!" is the best advice that she
can offer; then she goes on like Bion's old man, "in time, this
bird that now eludes you will come without your thinking
about it"—

> Comme une jeune et tendre queste,
> Et foullant de ses piedz ta teste,
> Que c'est que d'aimer t'aprendra.

She is correct in a way, for love swoops down on the unsus-
pecting. "Instat semper Amor supra caput," writes Proper-

---

[13] "Discours d'une Maquerelle," *Œuvres*, ed. Courbet (Paris, 1875), pp.
176–81.

[14] R. V. Merrill, "Eros and Anteros," *Speculum*, XIX (1944), 265–84.

tius; [15] and he complains that the passion is both "furor" [16] and "insanus." [17] So if love brings madness and insanity, it is quite right that the birds of Bion and Ronsard perch on the lover's head. But Ronsard's old woman uses the word *fouler* and adds "ses piedz." This is a far rougher landing than Bion's "καθίξειο." The reason for this is not far to seek. Black thinking about love had competed with the brightness of Hellenic joy. There is an Eros who tramples his victims; he is styled "saevus"; and his triumphs are in the literary annals.

The cruelty of Eros is described as early as the fourth chorus of Sophocles' *Antigone*, and the full brutality of victorious Love is recounted in Ovid's *Amores*.[18] Love is, indeed, a dire actor. He may do what he wishes. He is never punished except in the imagination of poets, and then only in another world. The "Cupido Cruciatur" of Ausonius and the "Amor Victus Somno" of Modestinus, poems that show Eros repaid in his own silver, are both dreams that take place in the birdless land of Avernus. Their importance rests in the fact that the *topos* of the *registre des amoureaux* begins with them. It is interesting, too, that the angry *martyres* who have it out with Love are all women—Phaedra, Scylla, Medea, Procne, Dido, Ariadne, Thisbe—and all ghosts in the dark realm. These unhappy ladies become part of the long procession of the *martyres d'Amour* and as such they are well known before the end of the Middle Ages. "Au fort martir on me devra nommer,/ Se dieu d'Amour fait mulz amoreaux saints," writes Charles d'Orleans. "And rad also ful often in my contemplatyff medytacons," says the author of *The Mass of Venus*, "the holy legende of Martyrs of Cupydo." [19] The register

[15] II.xxx.7.
[16] I.i.7.
[17] I.ix.16.
[18] I.ii.19–28.
[19] The French expressions are collected in I. Siciliano, *François Villon* (Paris, 1934), pp. 313–36. For the English, see *The Lay-Folk's Mass-Book*,

grew longer, the number of sad martyrs increased as each new generation enrolled more broken lovers on the book. The whole topic was enlarged and annotated for the Renaissance by the truest of true lovers, Francesco Petrarch, in his "Trionfo d'Amore."

Petrarch's "Trionfo" looks back to the classics, to Dante, and to his own *Africa* for many of its tropes and images. In the *Africa*'s sixth book, Sophonisba, condemned to Hades as a suicide but pardoned by the good offices of Aeacus, enters the field of lovers and sees the martyrs wandering in the valley of shades. Her experience is repeated by the poet in the proper language of Tuscany:

> Vidi un'vittorioso e sommo duce.
> Pur com'un di color che'n Campidoglio
> Trionfal carro a gran gloria conduce.[20]

The trampling triumpher of this poem is familiar—a young man, proud and fierce of face ("garzon crudo"), who is nude, winged, and weaponed. The martyrs of love surround him: "parte occisi;/Parte feriti da pungenti strali." [21] The valley through which he rides is the valley of the shadow, a dark circle of the Inferno; and all of us are certain where we are when one of the chained prisoners, "un' ombra, alquanto men che l'altre trista" [22] approaches the unknowing Petrarch and tells him about Eros, "mansueto fanciullo, e fiero veglio." The line of martyrs moves through the succeeding books of the poem,

---

ed. Simmons (London, 1879), pp. 394-95. In Hoccleve's "Letter of Cupid" —a version of Christine of Pisa's "L'Epistre au Dieu d'Amours"—Cupid uses the expression "In my legende of Martres" (*Works,* ed. Furnivall [London, 1892], p. 85). The theme of Love as Death, which is also found in Cavalcanti, is expressed by Ronsard and by Guillaume Alexis (*Œuvres,* ed. Piaget and Picot [Paris, 1896], I, 24).

[20] "Triumphus Cupidinis" 1.13-15.
[21] *Ibid.,* 29-30.
[22] *Ibid.,* 40.

and, as they pass, the ghost "less sad than the rest" reads the *registre des amoureaux* and recites their fates. It is this book that the "vielle mere" (who is probably mentioned therein) has in mind when she warns the boy.

It must be confessed that when we reach the end of Ronsard's poem, our veins are less warmed and our sensibilities less charmed than when we had only Bion's poem in our emotional history. Love has become somewhat distasteful. It is associated with birds of ill-omen, with witchcraft, wounds, and bitter hearts. The delicate tradition invented by some of the Greeks is worn and tarnished. Eros has been expelled from the Christian Church; Cephalus has got a bishopric; and the terrestrial Cupid has made his bed in Hell.[23] But to return again to Anteros, the Renaissance "old ploughman" and "vielle mere" in one.

The little god Anteros, who plays an almost protective rôle in Ronsard's "Magie," appears also in the part of the cursed old man of Du Bellay's "L'Anterotique." His birth date was later than that of Eros, so the fact that the Renaissance thought of him as an old man may have had another sanction.[24] The classical conception of him as a *deus ultor*, who saw to it that the passion inspired by Eros was returned and who avenged the loving-unloved, was clear enough; but in his other nature, he was sometimes brought forward as a fighting opponent

---

[23] It is hardly necessary to prove the point that some mediaeval men could regard Cupid as a demon, but the texts are interesting. St. Isidore puts him sternly in Hell: "Est enim daemon fornicationis" (VIII.xi.80); and Theodulf, the "Pindar" of Charlemagne, follows the same theme: "Est sceleratus enim moechiae daemon et atrox/ Ad luxus miseros, saeva barathra trahens" (*Carmina*, ed. Duemmler [Berlin, 1881], I, 543). In Gervais du Bus, *Le Roman de Fauvel*, Cupid and Venus are found in the company of "Fornicacion, Advoutire/ Viegnent la, tout sanz contredire/ Cupide vendra et Venus;/ De tel gent ne demeure nus" (ed. Langfors [Paris, 1919], p. 147).

[24] A figurine of an old man was identified as Anteros as early as the *Mythologia* of Gyraldus; it is published and discussed in Montfaucon, *L'Antiquité* (Paris, 1719), I, 184.

of Cupid, as a deity who preferred honor and virtue to love. Alciati describes him as disarming and binding his passionate brother,[25] and Marguerite of Navarre calls this violence an act of purification.

> Amour, remply de pitié et de zelle,
> D'amour mourant toucha la legiere aille,
> Et l'arracha du corps tendre et beau:
> La trousse print, et ses traicts avec elle,
> L'arc impiteux et la corde cruelle,
> Aussi l'espais et ignorant bandeau.
> Le tout il mit en un feu si nouveau
> Que leur chaleur il convertit en glace;
> Sans oublier de Venus le flambeau,
> Dont ce sainct feu toute navrure efface.[26]

But Anteros as the chaste opponent of Cupid was capable of disguises, and he assumes one of these in the "Cupido Conquered" of the subpoet Barnabe Googe.

Googe's poem, printed in 1563, is a vision poem in which the classical past is expressed in familiar mediaeval *formulae*. The poet, suffering from an amorous malady, wanders into a spring garden and falls asleep by a pool. In his dream he meets Mercury who escorts him to the Court of Diana, which is filled with those who were formerly on the *registre des amoureaux*. Then we learn that a hostile army is at the gates, and we go out to see the Cupid of Petrarch ride by in his chariot.

[25] In most editions of the *Emblemata* of Alciati, the CIXth emblem shows Anteros looking very much like Eros but without his identifying attributes. He is described as the god who draws men's minds on high. The CXth emblem shows him tying disarmed Eros to a tree. In Belleau's "Contre l'Amour," the poet assumes the part of Anteros and defies the god, saying of love, "Il vient de nous, mais las! pour voiler mieux/ De nostre mal la trop folle entreprise,/ Nous voulons bien que ce Dieu favorise/ Nostre malheur d'un tiltre glorieux" (*Œuvres*, ed. Marty-Laveaux [Paris, 1878], I, 171–72).
[26] *Les Dernières Poésies*, ed. Lefranc (Paris, 1896), p. 301.

The Captaine chyfe in Charyot ryde
   with Pompe and stately Pryde:
With Bow in hand of glistering gold,
   and Quyver by his syde.
Wher many a shaft full sharp doth ly:
   and many a mortall Darte,
That hath with poysoned force destroid,
   Full many a yealdyng Harte.[27]

The army of Diana, commanded by "Hipolitus," takes the field, and the battle begins. Cannons blaze and arrows fly. Idleness, Cupid's Ovidian captain, is slain; then "Hipolitus" kills Cupid's charioteer and captures the god. At this point Googe wakes up, but once again Cupid is conquered in a dream. "Hipolitus" becomes Anteros in this particular action, but one must also recall that his Greek predecessor, Hippolytus, had a prominent place among the martyrs of love.

This is the poetical background to Spenser's March eclogue, and I should like to summarize it before I approach the poem. Bion provides us with graceful instruction on the nature of love as first seen by an adolescent boy, but he brings into the pleasant wood of birdsong the amused but cold voice of the old farmer. Among other Greeks and Romans, the god who is also a bird becomes fierce of claw and beak; he begins to resemble the feathered hawk described by Passerat, a French contemporary of Spenser:

                    Cupidon me devore:
   Et ma chair, et mes nerfs, et mes os, et ma peau
   Sont tousiours deschirez par ce cruel oiseau.[28]

This other Eros is a destroyer and a trampler of lovers who can only work their revenge on him through wishful dreams. He is also a disease, as classical physicians testified, that re-

[27] *Eglogs, Epytaphes and Sonettes,* ed. Arber (London, 1910), p. 118.
[28] *Poésies,* ed. Blanchemain (Paris, 1880), I, 58.

quires witchcraft for cure or satisfaction. His insulting triumphs continue throughout the Middle Ages, and he makes
martyrs by the score, but they hardly await beatification, for
their god has descended to Hell. Much of this evil is gathered
up in Ronsard's poem in which Love is a bird of prey, an
angel with a dimmed aureole. From the whole literary tradition,
not from two poems slavishly imitated, comes the March
eclogue. This poem of Spenser's is a fragment of tradition
as is the *Shepheardes Calender,* and unless we see it as part of
the great whole, we shall never know its plain import.

We must first understand the timelessness posited by the
poet for the whole work. It is not just a calendar for one year;
it is a perpetual one. "Loe I have made a Calendar for every
year," says Spenser in his epilogue. But though it is a calendar,
it is also a compendium of a young poet's experience and
thought. Spenser, a recent graduate of Cambridge, stands like
the Renaissance Hercules at the choice of ways, but what had
once seemed clear to him is now misted over by his first experiences with maturity. Like the boy birdcatcher, he, too,
has glimpsed love as a life choice, but love, if the testimony of
the whole poem may be believed, has played him false. "E.
K.," the mysterious annotator of the *Calender,* makes this
clear for us:

> Onely this appeareth, that his unstayed yougth had long
> wandred in the common Labyrinth of Love, in which time to
> mitigate and allay the heate of his passion, or els to warne (as
> he sayth) the young shepheards. s. his equalls and companions
> of his unfortunate folly, he compiled these xii. Æglogues. . . . [29]

The "unfortunate folly" of love dominates the eclogues for
January, March, June, and August; and in the first and third

---

[29] *The Works of Edmund Spenser,* ed. E. Greenlaw, C. Osgood, F. Padel-
ford, and R. Heffner (Baltimore, 1943), I (*Minor Poems,* ed. C. Osgood
and H. Lotspeich), 10.

of these poems, Colin, who is at once both the hero of the whole poem and the poet himself, is the dominant speaker. March and August are, I think, special glosses on the other two poems that present the love tragedy of Colin and its consequent melancholia. The December eclogue echoes the tone of the eclogue for January and concludes with a renunciation of love: "Tell *Rosalind,* her *Colin* bids her adieu."

An anti-eroticism stains all the love eclogues. The poet is very young so he can talk of love as a passion with which he is finished. The god-bird has, indeed, trampled on his head. The experience of both Greek and French boys has been his, and the cynical advice of the "vielle mere" has proved correct. Even in the November eclogue, where the beloved Dido is the subject of his song, she is obviously a martyr of love, "Dead and lyeth wrapt in lead." For this reason, the love theme which begins in January, so that the rage of winter and the wasted world can be compared to the poet's heart, ends with December, when "The fragrant flowres, that in my garden grewe,/ Bene withered, as they had bene gathered long." Love-despair begins the poem and ends it. The January and December eclogues are soliloquies spoken by Colin-Spenser, but he also appears in November with Thenot, the traditional *senex,* who reproves the less sensitive Cuddie of February: "Thou art a fon of thy love to boste/ All that is lent to love wyll be lost." We see him again in June with Hobbinol, the contented middle-aged shepherd, who has found the Paradise "whych Adam lost." His attitude is reasonably constant; life is desperate, love fleeting, art unrewarding. In January he breaks his pipes; in December he forswears love. These were his immediate hopes; they are now his intense disappointments. The other eclogues examine at a distance the secondary problems of the young man's life.

When we turn to March, we discover, thanks to Professor

Spitzer,[30] that Bion's old man and Ronsard's "mere" have become the second story, the lesser story that is told offhandedly. When Eros was a young bird, Willye's father,

> him caught upon a day,
> (Whereof he wilbe wroken)
> Entangled in a fowling net,
> Which he for carrion Crowes had set,
> That in our Peeretree haunted.
> Tho sayd, he was a winged lad,
> But bowe and shafts as then none had:
> Els had he sore be daunted.

Willye's father seems to have escaped, to have had a better fate than Thomalin; but is he really free? There is at home, according to Willye, "A stepdame eke as whott as fyre." It seems as if the "vielle mere" has crossed the waters from France to be the second wife of the ploughman, who has lost his Amaryllis. Eros has been "wroken." It is the case—not unknown in literature—of the bird and the birdcatcher reversing rôles, a theme which begins with Petrarch's

> Amor fra l'erbe una leggiadra rete
> D'oro e di perle tese sott'un ramo
> Dell' arbor sempre verde ch' i' tant' amo,
> Ben chè n'abbia ombre più triste che liete.[31]

But it is Thomalin who is the major character of the March eclogue, and, in spite of the parallels, his is a totally new story. In some ways he is a fitting center because, as we learn in the July eclogue, he is a young man of high religious sensitivities, who suffers as much over the wounds of the shepherds' church as he does over those of love.

[30] "Spenser, Shepheardes Calendar, March ll.61–114, and The Variorum Edition," SP, XLVII (1950), 494–505.

[31] Le Rime, ed. Mestica (Florence, 1896), p. 260. On the theme of the net-layer caught, see Lorenzo d'Medici, Opere, ed. Simioni (Bari, 1913), I, 163; Baif, Œuvres, ed. Marty-Laveaux (Paris, 1881), I, 97; O. de Magny, Souspirs, ed. Courbet (Paris, 1874), p. 8.

The March eclogue begins on a day with a hint of spring in it; and Willye and Thomalin, who have been noticing the evidences of the new life—the starting grass, the nesting swallow, the clearing skies—ponder the end of "winters sorowe." The accumulated suggestions of the gay season are made into an aria by Willye.

> *Flora* now calleth forth eche flower,
> And bids make ready *Maias* bowre,
> That newe is upryst from bedde.
> Tho shall we sporten in delight,
> And learne with Lettice to wexe light,
> That scornefully lookes askaunce,
> Tho will wee little Love awake,
> That now sleepeth in *Lethe* lake,
> And pray him leaden our daunce.

The "little Love" whom Willye talks about is not the devastating Eros, who destroys the body and the mind; he is the sort of love that invests the body during the warmer weather for a day. Neither of the shepherds is exactly an innocent adolescent; they are more mature than Bion's "κυρος" and Ronsard's "enfant." Willye has had some previous experience with this sort of love; he calls it "sport" and adumbrates the remarks that Milton's fallen but inexperienced Adam makes to his facile consort Eve. Lettice is for him a charming animal; now she looks "askaunce," but her season will come. The fleshly nature of his springtime infatuations is supported by "E. K's" gloss on the subject of Flora, once a Roman harlot, who was made by the Latins into a "Goddess of floures."

Thomalin, we can imagine from our insight into his puritan nature, began as an opponent of love. He, too, may have once thought of passion as a seasonal matter—it came when the sap rose—and this attitude may have put him off guard. Now he knows better: "lustie love still sleepeth not,/ But is abroad at his game." He has gone into the wood, into the field of life;

but he has not gone as a boy birdcatcher. He has entered the world as an aggressive hunter, bearing bow and quiver. He sees a bush move and discharges an arrow. He knows that the quarry is not a nightingale or a wood thrush, but greater game, "faerie, feend, or snake." When the god shines forth, he needs no old man nor sullen ancient hag to warn him. He knows whom he faces. There is also no question of catching the bird, of securing another specimen for his aviary. Thomalin assumes the nature of the Renaissance Anteros; he "levelde againe/ And shott at him with might and maine,/ As thicke, as it had hayled." His purpose is clear; he is the avenger of the martyrs of love; he will strike Eros down. The nature of this god is also plain. He is not a bird on the bough; he has grown too large for the pear tree (the lecherous perch) where Willye's father bagged him. He is now of man's size, and he appears among the "lasciva hedera," the "wanton ivy" that we know so well.[32]

Thomalin's darts are swiftly exhausted, and he throws

[32] The "wanton ivy" is a definite symbol for Spenser. When Venus invades the dream of the Red Cross Knight and brings the false Una, Flora crowns the phantom with "yuie garland" (I.1.48). The Bower of Acrasia is "Framed of wanton Yuie, flouring faire" (II.5.29), and her phallic fountain is covered with a golden vine of imitation ivy, which "Low his lascivious armes adown did creepe" (II.12.41). The covert in the Garden of Adonis where Venus meets her paramour is shaded by trees that are knit together "with wanton yuie twine entrayld athwart" (III.6.44). It is hardly surprising to meet Lust clad only in "a wreath of yuie greene" (IV.7.1–2). Ivy patronized by Bacchus and hence associated in Spenser as in antiquity with drunkards and gluttons was made wanton when Theocritus transferred it to Priapus. The god is represented, his head bound with ivy and crocuses, creeping round the bed of the sleeping Daphne (Epigrammata 3). Catullus shows us a lover going to his nuptial bed with love chaining his mind as the ivy winds about a tree (Carmina LXI.31–35), and Horace gave Spenser the proper adjective: "Omnes in Damlin putris/ Deponent oculos, nec Damalis novo/ Divelletur adultero,/ Lascivis hederis ambitiosior" (Carmina I.36.20–23). It should also be noted that the mouth which makes the entrance to Alma's House is "cast" over with a "wandring vine/ Enchaced with a wanton yuie twine."

"pumie stones" with little effect. Suddenly he knows that he is lost, that flight is his only safety. He ends his career as Anteros and assumes the crown of a martyr. Eros does not trample on him; this is a special honor reserved for Love's servants. The fate of Thomalin is to be worse because the arrow that Cupid shoots hits him in the heel and not in the heart. This strange change of target would perplex us, indeed, if "E.K." did not supply us with an enlightening gloss, the spiritual reading, as a mediaeval man might say, of Spenser's literal text. The shot that Paris, the ancestor of lascivious Paridell, fired at Achilles and the inflicted wound are, "E.K." writes, expressions of lustful love. But, as he explains, the head of the arrow cut those veins that lead "to the previe partes" and hence "the partie straighte becommeth cold and unfruiteful which reason our Poete wel weighing, maketh this shepheards boye of purpose to be wounded by Love in the heele." When Eros is opposed, he can become Anteros. He can transform, by a pull on his bowstring, a young hunter into an old ploughman. Thomalin, wounded by Love at the entrance to spring, lives still in "the winter sorowe."

There is no question that Spenser's March eclogue abandons the simple charm of Bion's poem and embodies the melancholy sickness of Ronsard. The "enfant" has reached manhood; the dire predictions of the witch have matured in a frightening way. The sensitive shepherd has learned a great deal about the nature of love, and what he has learned is both a poetic explanation of the malady of Colin-Spenser and an apologia for his cold Decemberish rejection of love.

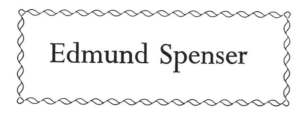

CHAPTER TWO

Edmund Spenser

"Muiopotmos, or The Fate of the Butterflie"

The tradition that helps in the reading of the March eclogue enables us to discover a moral meaning in the "Muiopotmos." When the poem is read literally, it is delicate in fancy, suggesting an Alexandrian intaglio in which the elaborateness of execution makes up for the slenderness of theme. But when we read Spenser's poem for a second time, we are convinced that it has a meaning more serious than it seems to have; and though some early readers of the poem described it as an imaginative exercise in the mock-heroic mode, a charming predecessor of Drayton's "Nymphidia," others saw behind the literal screen a serious purpose. One critic saw in it a Keatsian contention between Youth and Death; another thought it a poem about "the fate of a dreamer"; others contend that it is an allegory of the poetic nature and that it is associated in some way with Spenser's notions of his own poetic powers.

More recently the poem has been anatomized by historians who have found in it some fragment of Tudor history, something about court or political rivalry, some morsel of backstairs gossip. We are informed by them that the poem is a secret account of the relations between Spenser and Lady Carey, Raleigh and Essex, Spenser and Burghley, Sidney and Oxford, or Burghley and Essex. All of these historical interpretations are hung like delicate but withering garlands on the seemingly confusing implications of the first and second stanzas. Now the first stanza informs us that we shall hear of "deadly dolorous debate. . . . / Betwixt two mightie ones of great estate," who were drawn into "armes, and proofe of mortall fight" through hate and ambition. Neither of the two antagonists, Spenser continues, could endure the scorn of the other, and hence "from small iarre/ Their wraths at length broke into open warre." The second stanza, which is probably disconnected from the first, is used by Spenser to ask the Muse Melpomene to "reveale" to him the "roote" and "tragicall effect," and to "detect" the "meanes," through which Clarion declined "to lowest wretchednes." To these opening stanzas Spenser seems to have appended a poem of more than four hundred lines that completely forgets (unless an historical fact is read into the literal) all of the first stanza.

My own reaction to the first stanza is to ask whether or not Clarion or Aragnoll have the necessary attributes to be "mightie ones." And I am unable to discover that Clarion ever realizes that Aragnoll is his mortal enemy. As a matter of poetic fact, the very opposite of this is flatly stated a moment before the butterfly falls victim to the spider.

> Suspition of friend, nor feare of foe,
> That hazarded his health, had he at all. (377–78)

There is certainly no combat between the two symbolic
insects, no "small iarre," no "open warre," no "wraths" except
that of Aragnoll. We are told that Clarion is Aragnoll's
"hated foe" (254), and Spenser supplies a pair of myths to
expound this hate; but nowhere in the poem is it openly announced that Clarion, the hero, knows anything about the
potential danger to himself. In fact, Aragnoll seems not too
busy about his personal revenge; shortly before he saw the
butterfly in the garden, he was impartially contemplating
"How he might anie in his trap betray" (248). A particular
revenge on Clarion is really not his primary intent; he is
ready for any victim he can snare. Quite plainly, almost
everything that Spenser says in the first stanza is flatly denied
by the poem as a whole.

Spenser, as we know, is a forgetful poet; yet it is hard to
believe that, having written the first stanza, he would immediately put it out of his mind. Because of the troubling
nature of these opening lines, the whole poem has been read
by several critics as recreation in the manner of Vergil's
"Culex"; and though we might wonder whether Spenser
read Vergil's poem in this fashion, it is not impossible that
he intended a playful meaning for the "Muiopotmos." The
mock-heroic is not, however, an Elizabethan literary fashion.
Spenser did not know the literary rules laid down for it by
Boileau, Le Bossu, and Scarron. This mode was only popular
after his time and was founded, I think, on a calculated mis-
reading of the opening lines of the *Iliad*.

Should Spenser have wanted to write a mock-epic, he
would probably have recalled the straightforward introduc-
tion to the "Culex": "Lusimus, Octavi, lusimus . . . ut historiae per ludum." Here is no pretense to grandeur; it is all
fun, as Vergil honestly remarks; it is a vacation from the
Muses of serious poetry. "Doctrina, vaces licet." A glance at
the opening phrases of "Virgil's Gnat" will suggest how

closely Spenser heard the Roman voice. A second model that would come to his mind is the pseudo-Homeric *"βατραχο-μυομαχια."* At the beginning of this poem, the Muses are summoned to sing a theme fit for Mars, to tell the giant deeds of frogs and mice, deeds comparable to those of the Titans: *"μιμούμενοι ἔργα Γιγάντων."* This induction is rightly ironic, but the poem that succeeds it fits the promise of. the preface even though the fit is tight. With the opening lines of these two ancient mock-epics, the "Muiopotmos" has nothing in common; for this reason and because of what I read in the poem, I am ready to believe that the key stanza was solemnly intended.

The second stanza, on the other hand, is more closely adjusted to the action of the poem, and it probably should not be read as a continuation of the first stanza. "The roote whereof and tragicall effect" does not necessarily conjoin "open warre," although it is usually read as a poetical appendage. It could, in fact, be grammatically self-contained and its purpose might well be the exposition of Clarion's tragedy. The grammatical unity becomes clearer, and typographical blurring may be avoided, if the difficult stanza is rewritten with a transposed line:

> Vouchsafe, O thou the mournfulst Muse of nyne,
> That wontst the tragick stage for to direct,
> In funerall complaints and wayfull tyne,
> Reveale to me, and all the meanes detect
> The roote whereof and tragicall effect,
> Through which sad *Clarion* did at last declyne
> To lowest wretchedness; and is there then
> Such rancour in the harts of mightie men?

In this form the stanza is aloof from its predecessor; and since we have difficulty in thinking of either the butterfly or the spider as "mightie ones," there could be some other opponents

implied whose traditional quarrel brought on the murder
of Clarion. Rancor is a trait of uncontrolled passion that fits
the nature of Aragnoll, but the whole statement is also a
kind of afterthought that reduces to the human level a mental
disturbance experienced on a higher plane.

There are two well-known classical myths brought together in the "Muiopotmos," and by scanning them we
may find the moral translation of "mightie ones." The poem
itself depends to a great degree on these myths, and so we
cannot regard them as simply ornamental. The first myth
is that of Venus and Astery, a legend that Spenser invents by
combining the story of Cupid and Psyche with that of Jupiter
and Asteria. The myth that Spenser remakes from these is
that Astery, the most charming of Venus's nymphs, made her
companions so jealous they complained to the goddess that
Cupid had aided the girl in a flower-gathering contest. When
she heard of this aid, Venus gathered old fears as Astery
gathered "the children of the spring,"

> Not yet unmindfull, how not long agoe
> Her sonne to *Psyche* secrete love did beare,
> And long it close conceal'd, till mickle woe
> Thereof arose, and manie a rufull teare. (130–33)

She gave the girl the form of the butterfly, a pleasanter
metamorphosis than that of the classical Asteria. The second
important myth, with necessary innovations, is the more
familiar one of Minerva and Arachne; it blends with the first
legend to explain the difficult stanza and weave the subtle
web of the "Muiopotmos."

The Venus of the first myth, recalling her former domestic
difficulties with Psyche, whom she persecuted because the
innocent beauty of the girl brought about a decline in her
own cult, decides on this occasion to take no risks, for she
has a "iealous feare" of a repetition of the old disaster. She

promptly transforms her erstwhile favorite, who had gathered flowers so well, into a butterfly infatuate of blossoms. The butterfly comes into being because of the goddess's fear and envy. In the second myth, Arachne is changed into a spider through her own impious pride, but Minerva effects this metamorphosis, not because of jealous fear but out of reasonable pity. The pity of the wise goddess is thus contrasted with the jealousy of the sensual one. Clarion flits between the two myths when Spenser revises the Ovidian legend by making Minerva a patroness-general of butterflies. The goddess, according to his invention, places a butterfly among the leaves of her peaceful olive when she ties the final knots in her weaving. The butterfly begotten of Venus's jealousy and the unjust punishment of an innocent nymph is adopted by Minerva as the supreme symbol of her skill in her art; it seems to flutter and shine and is almost alive in wool. When the competing Arachne sees it, she knows that she is beaten. This is the reason for Aragnoll's hatred of Clarion, according to the Spenserian text; the spider sees in the butterfly the ensign of his mother's defeat. Since their competitions with mortals (Psyche and Arachne) recall it, we also may remember that the two goddesses were ancient rivals.

The mythographers whom Spenser read take us back to the famous contest between Juno, Minerva, and Venus for the golden apple of Eris (daughter of Nemesis of the first stanza), a legend well known in the Renaissance but one that Spenser never retells. From this contention and the decision of Paris came the war between the Greeks who were favored by Juno and Minerva, and the men of Troy who were supported by Venus. If it is a reasonable act of interpretation to pass by association from clear myths to hidden ones, we may have the meaning of the bothersome first stanza. The names of Venus and Minerva may be substituted for "the two mightie ones of great estate." They were certainly drawn

into arms and mortal strife "through prowd ambition and hart-
swelling hate." The "small iarre" produced by Jar at the
marriage feast of Peleus and Thetis becomes the "open warre"
between the Greeks and the Trojans. A minor footnote to
this epic conflict is the "Muiopotmos," for, as Spenser's composed myths suggest, the butterfly is favored by Minerva
as the symbol of her triumph; but it is also the sign of
Venus's irrational jealousy. The links of the chain of causes
bind the death of Clarion to the apple of Eris. Stanza one
may contain the great antecedents; stanza two, the proposi-
tion of the immediate poem.

The literal reading of the "Muiopotmos" may now be
made with a certain assurance. The butterfly Clarion, unaware
of his symbolic history and of the great cause between Venus
and Minerva, is slain by the spider who is well tutored in
traditional antipathy. A conflict on high affects the humble
ones below. The moral may be pondered: when great men
or goddesses quarrel, lesser innocents suffer. This may be all
that the poem means; but I am inclined to think that it has
a higher seriousness than this, that it is an allegorical account
of the eternal struggle between Good and Evil, and, on a
subordinate plane, between Wisdom and Pleasure as partisans
of these great forces. To discover this seriousness we can
make an excursion into the history of the legend of Cupid
and Psyche to which Spenser alludes.

The legend of Cupid and Psyche came to the Renaissance
through the *Metamorphoses* of Apuleius, but it had first
passed through the Middle Ages where it was converted into
an allegory of the human soul. The apotheosis of Psyche at-
tracted Martianus Capella,[1] who states that Psyche was born
divine because she was the daughter of Entelechia and Apollo;
he adds that she was endowed with the diadem of immortality

[1] *De Nuptiis Philologiae et Mercurii,* ed. Dick (Leipzig, 1955), pp. 6–9.

by Jupiter, given a fillet by Juno, a robe by Minerva, and other symbolic gifts by other divinities. She was denied as a bride to the postulant Mercury because she was already wed to Eros. The handsome story first told by the Platonist Apuleius was thus made into an Aristotelian legend.

The pseudo-Fulgentius (thought by the Renaissance to be a contemporary of Martianus) gave the story Christian meaning for "those who do not read it falsely." His account is as follows:

> Those who read rightly will consider the city in which Psyche lives as the world, and they will see in her parents, the King and Queen of the city, God and Matter. They will also assume that Psyche and her two elder sisters are Flesh, Liberty (or Free-Will), and the Soul, for the Greeks call the soul *Psyche*. They will also want Psyche to be the youngest, because, as we know, the body is made first and then the soul is added. She is naturally the most beautiful of the three sisters, because she is superior to Liberty and more noble than Flesh. Venus or Libido envies her and sends Cupid to destroy her. But there is a desire (cupiditas) of good as well as of evil, so Cupid is charmed by the Soul and mingles with it in union, persuading it not to look at his face, that is, not to learn the delights of desire. So Adam, though he saw, did not see that he was nude until he ate of the tree of desire. So the Soul did not agree at first with her sisters, Flesh and Liberty, in their wish to learn Love's face, but, finally, moved by their continuous demands, she uncovered the lamp, which is the hidden flame of desire burning in the breast. Seeing that his face was comely, she loved beyond reason, The droppings of the lamp are said to have burned him, because all desire, the more it loves, the more it burns and stains the flesh with the mark of sin. So, desire made bare, the Soul is deprived of her powerful fortune, cast into dangers, and expelled from her royal house.[2]

[2] *Expositio Sermonum Antiquorum*, in *Auctores Mythographi Latini*, ed. Van Staveren (Leyden, 1742), pp. 715–20.

After these allegorical readings, the legend of Cupid and Psyche slept soundly during most of the Middle Ages,[3] to come wide awake in Boccaccio's *Genealogy of the Gods.* Boccaccio admittedly read an ancient myth as if he were a mediaeval theologian.[4] With a sense of the four interpretations to sustain him, Boccaccio retells the story of Cupid and Psyche and summarizes Martianus's reading; then, lifting the literal cloth, he finds the moral meaning on the bare boards of the story. Psyche is without question the human soul, the daughter of the Sun, of God, who is the true light of the world and the creator of the rational spirit. Her two sisters

[3] M. Kawczynski, "Ist Apuleius im Mittelalter bekannt wesen?" in *Bausteine zur Romanischen Philologie* (Halle, 1905), pp. 193–210. Apuleius came to the Renaissance with an impressive testimony behind him. His Renaissance biographers, Beroaldus and Wowerius, describe his reputation as a magician, which had earlier been emphasized by Lactantius in the *Divinae Institutiones* (*PL*, VI, 558) and by Augustine in letters to Marcellinus and Deogratias (*Epistolae* [*PL*, XXXIII, 383, 583]). In the *De Civitate Dei*, Augustine elevates Apuleius to the ranks of the Platonists and describes him as the best philosopher in Greek and Latin (VIII.12.14). He is commended by Bessarion for defending Plato, in *In Calumniatorem Platonis* (Venice, 1516), pp. 4–4v. He was read by Ficino and cited in the *Symposium*, in *Opera* (Lyons, 1548), p. 280. The only Renaissance mythographer, as far as I know, to record the legend of Cupid and Psyche besides Boccaccio is Gyraldus. See his *Historiae Deorum*, in the *Opera* (Leyden, 1696), I, 406. For histories of the myth in western literature and art, see: Harriet Blake, *Classical Myth in the Poetic Drama of the Age of Elizabeth* (Lancaster, Pa., n.d.), pp. 49–60; Alice Nearing, *Cupid and Psyche by Shakerly Marmion* (Philadelphia, 1944), pp. 11–95; B. Stumfall, *Das Märchen von Amor und Psyche in seinem Fortleben in der französischen, italienischen, und spanischen Literatur bis 18. Jahrhundert* (Naumberg, 1907); U. de Maria, *La Favola di Amore e Psiche nella Letteratura e nell' Arte Italiana* (Bologna, 1899); J. M. de Gossio, *Fábulas Mitológicas en España* (Madrid, 1952), pp. 257–70; H. LeMaistre, *Essai sur le Mythe de Psyché dans la littérature française des origines a 1890* (Paris, 1950).

[4] *Della Genealogia degli Dei* (Venice, 1585), p. 8. Boccaccio here argues that pagan myths must be read according to their literal, moral, allegorical, and analogical senses. The same view was put forward by Ficino (*Opera* [Basel, 1576], p. 1370), and approved by Pico in *Heptaplus*, ed. Garin (Florence, 1942), I, 188.

are the vegetative and sensitive parts of the soul; consequently, Psyche is the youngest of the three because the rational soul is the last to develop. Her marriage to Cupid portrays the honest love of the soul for God, and she is carried to this love by Zephyr or the Vital Spirit. The prohibition of her lover against her seeing his face really expresses the unwisdom of attempting to learn the mysteries of theology. Now the two sisters—the lower two parts of the soul—are able to arrive at the lower limits of the rational soul's knowledge; but when they can go no further, they envy it. This is natural, for sensuality never accords with reason. The sisters now urge Psyche to look on her lord's face; they want her to use natural reason instead of the knowledge supplied by faith. They wish, also, to turn her from contemplation, to sow those seeds that bring weariness and no satisfaction. When she yields, she sees only the form of her lover; she sees the extrinsic works of God but not divinity, for no one can see God. Thus offending with her pride, she becomes disobedient and descends to the senses. The good of contemplation is totally lost; the divine marriage is dissolved. Penitent at last, Psyche wisely wishes the destruction of her sisters and sees to it that they have no power over reason. Purged of pride and disobedience, she comes once again to divine love and con-templation, is brought to eternal glory, and bears Love the child Pleasure, who is timeless beatitude.[5] In this fashion Boccaccio reads morally the story told by the old woman to Apuleius.

The myth of Cupid and Psyche, hallowed by the Platonic associations of its author, was read during the Renaissance as an allegory of the rational soul bound in marriage to Divine Love but disturbed in its marital duties by the lower levels of the mind. Martianus seems to have inaugurated the reading; the pseudo-Fulgentius elaborated it; and Boccaccio

[5] *Ibid.*, pp. 90v–92.

converted it to a spiritual narrative. None of these under-
standings of the myth lived in isolation from the others, for
with the *editio princeps* [6] of the *Metamorphoses* the wide
meadow of annotations surrounding it informs the reader
that the story has other meaning than the literal, and the
exegesis of these three allegorizers is either referred to or
reprinted. If Spenser had read Apuleius in an original text, he
would have learned from the margins what it meant in a
spiritual sense. It is not impossible, therefore, that this myth
is the key to a possible allegory hidden beneath the literal
text of the "Muiopotmos." The fate of the butterfly could
be the fate of the rational soul in a world where Evil and
Good contend for domination. Spenser's *fabula* can be a revision of the Psyche story. To make all of this a bit clearer,
I shall pass from Psyche to Clarion, the butterfly.

The Psyche legend, like that of the Phoenix, was one of
the few pagan myths accepted by early Christians. The
myth is represented on many Christian monuments, grave-
stones, catacomb frescoes, and sarcophagi; and the Christian
Psyche is usually painted with the wings of a butterfly.[7] The
reason for these symbolic wings is that the Greeks represented
the human soul as a butterfly. Now probably none of this
artistic tradition was known to Spenser, and the literary tradition that carries it to him is very thin. There are two poems
by Meleager in which that poet compares the enamoured soul
to a butterfly,[8] but I cannot believe that Spenser knew them.
When Dante describes the soul of man as a butterfly: "angelica
farfalla,/ Che vola alla giustizia senza schermi," [9] the older

---

[6] *Apuleius cum commento Beroaldi* (Venice, 1510); see the discussion of
the allegory on p. 8ov.
[7] M. Collingnon, *Essai sur les Monuments Grecs et Romains relatifs au
Mythe de Psyché* (Paris, 1877).
[8] *Anthol. Pal.*, V, 57; XII, 132.
[9] *Divina Commedia, Purg.* X.121–29.

scholiasts immediately recognize the symbol and explain it; [10] but there is no reason to believe that Spenser read Dante or his commentators. Though poets of the Italian Renaissance liked to compare lovers to butterflies circling a lamp,[11] I can find no evidence that they ever thought of the human soul as a butterfly. I do not think that the literary tradition is necessary in this instance to establish a connection; Spenser had only to look up the word for "soul" in any Greek lexicon such as the 1586 edition of Scapula's dictionary to read: "ψυχή, spiritus, flatus . . . Item papilio: apud Plut. symp. 2, prob. 3, & Aristot. hist. an. 1, 5, c. 19." I expect that any Renaissance man with "lesse Greeke" would have discovered this equivalence in the latter years of grammar school. So with this item of information we may attempt to explain the meaning of the "Muiopotmos." The poem is possibly about the rational soul, Clarion, the clear, the bright one. The butterfly hero may not be chosen by whim; the poem is no vacation from the Muse of serious verse.

Critics who have expounded the "Muiopotmos" in terms of "Virgil's Gnat" might do better to think in terms of the early books of the *Faerie Queene*, because the "Muiopotmos" could be an allegory of the wandering of the rational soul into error. The title, then, is not so ironic as it seems, for "πότμος," as Spenser surely knew, was reserved by the Greeks for the fatal destiny of great heroes: "πότμον ἐπισπεῖν," as Homer is accustomed to say. On the literal level there is irony, but it

---

[10] See the commentaries of Landino and Pietro di Dante in the edition produced by Biagi, Passerini, and Rostano (Turin, 1931). Benevenuto de Imola's commentary reads: "L'angelica farfalla, id est, papilionem, per quem intelligit animam rationalem, qui videtur de natura angelica celesti, quia immortalis, incorruptibiles, levis et pura" (*Comentum super Dantis Comoediam*, ed. Vernon [Florence, 1887], *ad loc.*).

[11] See the collection in Picinelli, *Symbolicus Mundi* (Cologne, 1687), I, 531–34.

washes away as the allegory unfolds. The clear soul, faultless
and sinless, sponsored by piety and wisdom (Minerva), yet
ballasted and weighed down by the senses (Venus), can come
through spiritual heedlessness into the web of evil. For this
tragedy, "πότμος" is an exact term and Melpomene the proper
Muse.

Clarion, when first we know him, is, while "heaven did
favour his felicities," no earthbound creature like Aragnoll;
he possesses the "Empire of the Aire." He is superior to all
other butterflies, the favorite of his father, who, we are told,
hopes that in time Clarion will be worthy of his paternal
heritage, "as should be worthie of his fathers throne." He is
not slothful, but joys to fly

> Through the wide compas of the ayrie coast,
> And with unwearied wings each part t'inquire
> Of the wide rule of his renowned sire. (38–40)

His flights of admiration above the clouds to the "Christall
Skie" in order to "vew the workmanship of heavens hight"
are counterpoised by his inspection of the watery surfaces
below. In Spenser's description of Clarion's active career of
admiring wandering there is a note of warning—Clarion
sometimes dares to "tempt the troublous winde." This is the
biography of Clarion before the tragedy begins, and it not
only contains certain suggestions of the flight of the rational
soul through the realm of creation but also hints at the
prospects of the spiritual inheritance of Christians who do
not succumb to curiosity.

This suggestion of an *hubris* in Clarion may mean no more
than the literal reading admits, and when I go beyond it,
I may be overreading; nonetheless, the enticing phrase, "troublous winde" has in it the suggestion of a traditional symbol.
If Spenser read an interpreted Bible, he would have found

the "wind" of Psalms 1:4 equated with inner temptation and the "wind" of Proverbs 11:4 with "spiritus malignus." [12] The "great wind from the wilderness" that smote the house in which Job's sons and daughters were eating and drinking (1:19) was clearly of diabolical origin, and glossators enlarged on the matter. When, for example, Garnerus wrote his chapter on the allegory of winds, he drew his first exemplary text from Job, but his summary heading for the essay makes the point clearer: in the Scriptures when "wind" is used in the singular, it means "the devil, hellish temptation, transitory good fortune, or pride"; in the plural "winds" means the souls of the holy.[13] Spenser uses the word in the singular. So Clarion's reckless tempting of the wind and the "ungracious blast out of the gate/ Of *Aeoles* raine," one of the possible causes of his fatal fall, may mean more than the letter states.

With the seventh stanza of the "Muiopotmos," we are present on a special summer day, a day so pleasant it seems impossible that any evil can blight its English charm. It reminds us of the day when the Red Cross Knight, proud in his new-found Christian virtues, met the windy Orgoglio. Clarion is about to venture forth, but the cautionary expression "with vauntfull lustie head" speaks disaster, for heedlessness, a false sense of security, and a failure to bridle the two lower sisters of the soul, will purchase his ruin. Before he goes forth, Clarion puts on his armor, and it is not unlike the gear recommended by St. Paul and rehearsed by Spenser in his letter to Raleigh. The breastplate is "pure substance"; and faith is "the substance of things hoped for." The helmet is of metal too rare for the metallurgists of this world, not Bilbo steel, not Corinth brass, not Orichalum. It is magically

[12] Rabanus Maurus, *Allegoriae in Sacram Scripturam* (PL, CXII, 1073–74).
[13] *Gregorianes* (PL, CXCIII, 51–56).

spiritual armor that can protect the wearer from bodily
wounds too. When Clarion is finally armed, he puts on
Psyche wings. The butterfly, or the soul, is ready.

The first flight of Clarion and the pleasures that the flight
brings are totally natural and Christianly decorous. Spenser,
by saying of them "That none gainsaid, nor none did him
envie" (151), stamps them with spiritual approval. By mid-
stanza, Clarion wavers from the true course and his tragic
flaw becomes apparent.

> The woods, the rivers, and the medowes green,
> With his aire-cutting wings he measured wide,
> Ne did he leave the mountaines bare unseene,
> Nor the ranke grassie fennes delights untride.
> But none of these, how ever sweete they beene,
> Mote please his fancie, nor him cause t'abide:
> His choicefull sense with everie change doth flit.
> Ne common things may please a wavering wit. (153–60)

With the last four lines of this stanza our fine estimate of
Clarion changes. The lower levels of his soul, the two gross
sisters of Psyche, take over; his flight of admiration becomes
a flight of idle curiosity.

The butterfly's "unstaid desire" now takes him to the
"gay gardins" where Art contends with Nature in an ominous
lavishness.[14] We know the garden that now attracts Clarion
from the world of legitimate natural pleasures; it is a sub-
division of Acrasia's Bower:

> whose faire grassy ground
> Mantled with greene, and goodly beautifide
> With all the ornaments of Floraes pride,

[14] One recognizes these gardens as Renaissance replicas of those sensual
pleasure places that the Middle Ages associated with the cult of Venus.
We recall *Le Roman de la Rose* (1323–1424), the poem of Flora and Phyllis
in the *Carmina Burana* (92.59–60), and the well-known witches' gardens in
Ariosto and Tasso.

> Wherewith her mother Art, as halfe in scorne
> Of niggard Nature, like a pompous bride
> Did decke her, and too lavishly adorne.[15]

Patterned after this garden of the fleshly way of life, the "gay gardins" where Clarion wanders are those in which Art aspires

> T'excell the naturall, with made delights:
> And all that faire or pleasant may be found
> In riotous excess doth there abound. (166–68)

The permissible world of experience is left behind, and Clarion yields to the senses. As yet he has not sinned, but his spiritual weakness will carry him into the web of evil. Spenser now begins to warn the reader, to suggest by adjectives that the butterfly-soul is in trouble. Clarion has a "curious busie eye" (171); he attempts to satisfy "his glutton sense" (179); he preys "greedily" (204) on the flowers, and then he rests in "riotous suffisaunce" (207). The hero, in spite of his Christian armor and the good hopes of his "Sire," is slipping into heedlessness. He is becoming more and more like Dante's "l'angelica farfalla."

> L'anima semplicetta, che sa nulla,
> Salvo che, mossa da lieto fattore,
> Volontier torna a ciò che la trastulla.
> Di picciol bene in pria sente sapore;
> Quivi s'inganna, e dietro ad esso corre,
> Se guida a fren non torce il suo amore.[16]

The poet Spenser, having suggested by plain statement that the butterfly-soul is curious, greedy, and uncontrolled, pauses in the direct narrative for an ironic excursion into the hedonist's doctrine.

[15] *The Faerie Queene* II.xii.50.
[16] *Purg.* XVI.88–93.

What more felicite can fall to creature,
Than to enjoy delight with libertie,
And to be Lord of all the workes of Nature,
To raine in th'aire from earth to highest skie,
To feed on flowres, and weed of glorious feature,
To take what ever thing doth please the eie?
Who rests not pleased with such happiness,
Well worthie he to taste of wretchednes. (209–16)

If this stanza stood by itself or if we did not read it with some care, we might feel that Spenser approved of Clarion's conduct in the "gay gardins." To the Christian reader, however, the whole passage is a meditation on destruction; it is almost a paraphrase of Satan talking to a rather simple victim. The worldly emphasis of the first line is seconded by the "delight with libertie" of the next. The butterfly-soul that cannot distinguish between "flowres" and "weed of glorious feature" will easily succumb to the eye-sins that hide behind "what ever thing doth please the eie." The Christian implications of this stanza are immediately bulwarked by the following one that comments on the transitoriness of existence, the mutability of all things, and the absurdity of fragile pleasures unless one is guided by "a God, or God." So Spenser warns against the lower life of the senses, and the phrase "a God, or God" establishes a religious tone on the foundations of both pagan and Christian morals.

It is just at this point, too, that Clarion is doomed, for we are instantly informed that Jove has woven the fate of the butterfly. "Heavens avengement," "πότμος," is at hand. Both Destiny and Providence are aware that the butterfly must fall. "Careles Clarion" (375) flutters sinward while Spenser provides us with two passages that comment on his "unstaid desire" and the heedless independence that is mutually possessed by the butterfly and the Red Cross Knight. Directed by desire, reckless Clarion feeds hither and yon in the garden of sensation,

> And whatso else of vertue good or ill
> Grewe in this Gardin, fetcht from farre away,
> Of everie one he takes. (201–203)

His inability on this fair morning to distinguish between good and evil, his love of foreign pleasures (any normal Englishman would see the fault in this), his eagerness to possess all that the spring brought forth comes, perhaps, from the spiritual vanity that ruined the Red Cross Knight. This suggestion is strengthened by a suite of lines that ushers in the actual tragedy,

> [Clarion] walkt at will, and wandred too and fro,
> In the pride of his freedome principall:
> Litle wist he his fatall future woe,
> But was secure, the liker he to fall.
> He likest is to fall into mischaunce,
> That is regardles of his gouvernaunce. (379–84)

This is a poetical restatement of the advice given by St. Paul to the men of Corinth, when he reminded the Church of the pride that brought Lucifer down and would overthrow them, too. "Let him that thinketh he standeth take heed lest he fall." Through heedlessness as much as through the "troublous winde," through pride of self-surety as much as through the hate of the spider, Clarion, brightest and fairest of souls, descends to the realm of the senses. With this fall, we return to a Christian reading of the Psyche myth.

It is time now, since the cue has been heard, for Aragnoll, son of Arachne and foe by tradition of Minerva's butterfly, to enter. Thanks to Job 8:14 (His trust shall be like the spider's web) and Isaiah 59:5 (They have eaten the eggs of asps and woven the webs of spiders), Aragnoll and his house embodied a Christian symbolism that associated them with impiety, heresy, hypocrisy, worldliness, and the very Devil himself. The web of the spider, says that great analogist Gregory,[17] "is like trust in hypocrites." Jerome[18] identifies the heretic with the spider, and Cyrillus[19] states that all impiety is like a web hung by a spider in an empty house. Origen[20] writes that the spider is the symbol of the sinner, and Petrus Blesensis[21] compares the insect to the foolish man of the world. An early commentary on the eleventh century *Physiologus* of Theobaldus combines all of these meanings into a spiritual discourse on the nature of Aragnoll.

> The Devil catches us as if we were flies; he is always putting traps, nets, and loops in our way so that he can take us through sin. When he takes someone in mortal sin, then he eviscerates and deprives them of grace unless the sinner is rescued by confession and penitence. So the chief snare of the devil is man's own will and it is only by repentance that he can avoid it. The spider fears the sun just as the devil fears the Holy Church and the just man, who can also be compared to the sun. Usually the spider weaves his web at night; so the devil weaves his when the just man is less watchful.[22]

Thus Aragnoll, the destroyer of the butterfly-soul, is unmasked.

What we now know about Aragnoll, we could have read out of his mother's legend. The ancients who knew her story saw it as another parable of a mortal who was foolish enough to challenge the power of the divine. When Spenser calls

[17] *Moralia in Job* (PL, LXXV, 845); echoed in the *Glossa Ordinaria* (PL, CXIII, 779–80).
[18] *Epistolae* (PL, XXII, 1174–75).
[19] *In Isaiam* (PG, LXX, 1308).
[20] *Commentarius in Psalmos* (PG, XII, 1408–1409).
[21] *Epistolae* (PL, CCVII, 60).
[22] Auber, *Histoire et Théorie du Symbolisme Religieux* (Paris, 1884), III, 496.

Arachne a "presumptuous Damzel," who "rashly dar'd" to compete with Minerva, he is simply carrying out the dictates of a long tradition. The fourteenth century *Ovide Moralisé* takes a similar attitude toward the story.

> Pallas, qui bien le veult gloser,
> Note devine sapience,
> Araigne fole outrecuidance,
> Qui ou dyable regne et maint,
> Et dou dyable l'ont or maint
> Qui ensivent sa discipline.
> Pallas, sapience divine,
> Fu corroucie et despit ot
> Dont Araigne la despitot,
> C'est li mondes musars et nices,
> Plains d'outrecuidance et de vices,
> Qui contre Dieu se vait ventent,
> N'a riens de cest siecle n'entent
> Fors aus oeuvres de vanité
> Et a confondre verité.[23]

This moral comment on the nature of Aragnoll's mother and her act of impiety was accepted by the later commentators, Giovanni del Vergilio[24] and Thomas Wallensis,[25] whose remarks were sometimes incorporated in editions of the *Metamorphoses* printed in the Renaissance. The dynasty of spiders had a moral and spiritual equivalence that Spenser could not avoid.

Spenser covers Aragnoll, at the very beginning of the poem, with satanic epithets. He is "a wicked wight," "foe of fair things," "author of confusion," "slave of spite." He builds a "hateful" mansion in which he lurks to "betray." He is

---

[23] Ed. de Boer, *Verhandelingen der Koninklijke Akademic van Weten-schappen, Afdeeling Letterkunde,* XXI (N.S., 1920), 298.

[24] For an account of his moralized Ovid, see Wicksteed and Gardner, *Dante and Giovanni del Vergilio* (Westminster, 1902), p. 321.

[25] *Metamorphoseos libri moralizati* (Lyons, 1513), ad loc.

filled with "poison." He has "malice" and a "false hart." He
is "deceitful" and plots "treason." At no point in the poem
is anything pleasant ever associated with this spider-Satan,
and this fact alone spoils the historical theories that identify
Aragnoll with some grand personage of the Elizabethan court.
Spenser fills his *Faerie Queene* with feckless knights, but there
is no reason to believe that he approved of fecklessness for
himself.

When Aragnoll is almost sunk under this freight of damna-
tion, two familiar similes are made with reference to him,
and once more he is associated with creatures of low moral
repute. We are told that he is like the fox stalking lambs, or
"a grimme Lyon rushing with fierce might." The first figure
is clear enough for any Christian reader, whereas the second
comes neatly from Psalm 21:22 (Save me from the mouth of
the lion) and I Peter 5:8 (because your adversary, the devil,
ranges round, a roaring lion). The Christian symbolists,
when it was fitting to do so, associated the lion with Hell.
"Evil spirits are called 'lions' because of their pride," [26]
writes Alanus de Insulis, an author not unknown to Spenser.
Faultless until then except for his heedlessness and his failure
to keep his lower senses in restraint, the butterfly-soul finally
falls into the web of impiety with Satan at its center. Spenser
has plotted the steps toward this fall, but he eventually gives
us the exact causes.

Clarion, Spenser says, is entangled in the web of impiety
because of "cruell Fate," "wicked Fortune," or an "ungracious blast out of the gate of *Aeoles* raine" (417–20). On
the Christian level, Fate, as Milton's God observes, can be
equated with Providence; and Fortune and the wind combine
to make the means by which Providence works. The wind
from "Aeoles raine" is a particularization of the "troublous
winde," which possessed a possible moral meaning. The moral

[26] *Elucidatio in Cantica Canticorum* (PL, CCX, 80).

interpretations of Vergil may make Spenser's meaning more clear. The story of Aeneas's experience with the winds of Aeolus is, of course, a major event in the *Aeneid,* and the humanists, who saw in Aeneas the pattern of the perfect man, made moral use of it. In a letter to Aretino, Petrarch announces that Aeneas is the human reason, and the winds that assail him are passions that afflict reason and that reason must control.[27] The philosopher Landino, who wrote a moral interpretation of the *Aeneid,* describes the epic as an allegory of the soul in search of divine wisdom or the Venus Urania. To this end, he writes, Aeneas or the soul flees from Troy (the vulgar Venus) and from its own sensuous nature (Paris) and embarks on a sea (life) fretted and disturbed by the storms of passion and desire.[28] It is not impossible that Spenser knew these moral equivalents of the wind symbol, and he may have expected us to read them into his literal statements.

It is not improper to read the "Muiopotmos" as a moral poem, as an account of the soul caught in the eternal struggle between reason and sensuality, between Good and Evil. The butterfly Clarion may exist to warn Spenser's readers about the nature of pleasure and self-confidence. The myth of the two insects is on a lower level than that of Cupid and Psyche but its ultimate purpose is probably the same. The universality of the moral is indicated by one of the final couplets that introduces the fate of the butterfly in tones recalling the greatest of tragedies.

> For loe, the drerie stownd is now arrived,
> That of all happiness hath us deprived. (415–16)

[27] *Opera* (Basel, 1554), p. 868.
[28] *Disputationes* (s.l., n.d.), fol. 4.

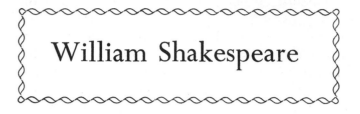

CHAPTER THREE

William Shakespeare

The Tempest

Though *The Tempest* is a play, it is also a complicated masque or a narrative poem with lyric intervals. It is difficult to compare with Shakespeare's other plays, for it is briefer, more elaborate in fantasy, and in some respects more intensely personal than they. During the last century, it was thought to be confessional and Prospero's final speeches were associated with Shakespeare's retirement from the theater. The play does not permit this conclusion. Shakespeare is not forsaking his art. If *The Tempest* is to be read biographically at all, it must be seen as a poetical summary of the poet's life and its satisfactory achievements, as the poetic rendering of that bright moment at the end allowed to men of special favor, a moment that assures them that what they have loved will endure. *The Tempest*, like *Pericles*, *Cymbeline*, and *The Winter's Tale*, is one of a series of warm afternoons in the late autumn of Shakespeare's life. It is mellow with the ripeness of knowledge, for its maker has discovered the right ritual for the marriage of the inner and the outer world, of the real and the ideal, the experienced and the imagined, the dream and the actuality.

With the writing of *Hamlet* Shakespeare begins to experiment with darkness, and the sun does not come again until Pericles, who is "music's master," hears, like no other character in Shakespeare's plays, the harmony of the heavenly spheres. This is the same harmonious end toward which Prospero looks: "When I have required/ Some heavenly music—which even now I do." It is plain from the tragedies that an awakening from idealism into cold reality is the required preliminary experience to the search for celestial harmony. The distaste for life expressed by Hamlet, a distaste that helps to shape the succeeding tragedies, has been associated by biographical critics with the poet's private experience, with his increasing boredom with life and art, with an obsessing puritanical temper, with a disappointment in love or friendship, and with some sort of neurotic illness. None of this can be proved. All we know is that Shakespeare experimented with tragedy and tragic despair; then, using the same sets of tragic circumstances, he led his creatures out of the world of darkness into eternal day.

In each of the three plays written before *The Tempest*, the dramatic premise is tragic, although the poet always forfends "the promised end." Pericles, a Hamlet-like seeker of truth, begins his search in a place evil with the reek of incest and carnage. He wanders through storm upon storm over the wide map of the great lost world of antiquity. In the end, he hears the divine music, sees the vision of the celestial "goddess argentine," and finds at last his lost wife and child. The play follows an established legend, but the bareness of myth is made a living reality through the poet's restored belief. *Cymbeline,* which is drawn from the truth of history, shuns history so that Cymbeline may see the consequence of wrong, that Imogen may triumph in her love, that the lost princes may be found, that Posthumus, cured and forgiven, may have his dream made real, and that Iachimo, weak son of Iago, may be pardoned. With *The Winter's Tale* the miracle increases, for Greene, father of the story, could not believe in the resurrection of Hermione or the redemption of Leontes. Shakespeare, the poet, is alone able to distract the current that flows toward tragedy. The end is so miraculous that we, too, like the healed King Leontes, may say, "If this be magic, let it be an art/ Lawful as eating." The ritual of restoration, the magic that transforms the stale world into the "brave new world," is presented to us in the last play, which interprets the mode of all these romances. We must go to *The Tempest* for this information and then we may understand what the wise, young poet Keats meant when he said that Shakespeare lived the life of allegory.

The Tempest, like the other last plays, is separated from the world of the Elizabethans by an imaginative reach that is greater than the finite measurements of space and time. It is remote in time and it is out of time. The imaginative distances are enhanced by the mortal chronology of the text: the precise three hours of the action and of the twelve-year island sojourn of Prospero and Miranda. Because of these exact statements the interior distance between us and the island is closer than are the external distances of time and space. We can almost find the island in the atlas of literary tradition: it is on or off the direct course to Carthage or Tunis, the capes where Aeneas, swept by storm, came into the realm of "widow Dido." The time may be any time, but it is more truly a constant present. All of these distinctions are made certain by the past, for it is not just that Shakespeare was an Englishman or read the sea adventures of Jourdan that put the island on the chart of his imagination.

We stand, at the play's beginning, watching a storm that we also see through the eyes of Prospero, the stormmaker, and of the admirable Miranda. It is a fairy storm, real only to the men returning from Carthage and to the spellbound girl. It is a storm similar to the one that Prospero may have known inwardly when twelve years before he and his infant daughter crossed the same waters on "a rotten carcass of a butt."

> There they hoist us,
> To cry to the seas, that roared to us; to sigh
> To the winds, whose pity sighing back again
> Did us but loving wrong.[1]

The storm that was then in Prospero's mind was not unlike the one that drove Lear mad, but now, except for occasional ripples of anger or impatience, it has blown itself out. Prospero has been tested and educated in his island; he has learned to control his passions' weather and so he can make storms in semblance. When Miranda asks how they came ashore, Prospero, grateful for the experience, can give her a serene answer, "By Providence divine." To reach this emotional shelter, one must pass through stormy weather to an island, and it is on the island, outside of known reality, that a symbolic miracle can occur.

To come across broad waters in a helpless boat and to find haven at last in a magic island is a symbolic motif that has found a place in the history of heroes since literature began. The storms that drove the Argonauts are poetically recorded; [2] we know in the same way the wracking tumult in

---

[1] I.ii.148–51.
[2] Apollonius of Rhodes, *Argonautica* IV.1228–1304; Valerius Flaccus I.574–607.

which Ceyx drowned [3] and the monstrous gale that brought
Aeneas to Carthage.[4] The accounts of the poets are sustained
by the romantic historians, one of whom, Diodorus Siculus,
gives us the tale of Iambulus, storm-driven for months in the
Erythraean Sea and brought at last to an island where men
lived happily in the earliest of Utopias.[5] The same romancer,
in his book of islands, sets down a legend congenial with that
of *The Tempest*. He writes that sailors from Carthage, ex-
ploring the sea beyond the Pillars of Hercules, were carried
by strong winds far into the ocean. After many days, they
were driven onto an island filled with springs, rivers, and
beautiful orchards but unknown to men. Its climate was so
felicitous that "it would appear . . . that it was a dwelling-
place of gods." [6] But the master of storm, of shipwreck, and
of enchanted islands is the wise son of Laertes, Odysseus of
many counsels. To understand part of the tradition behind
The Tempest, we should rehearse his Mediterranean journeys
and understand what they mean.

   The whole course of Odysseus from Troy to the high hall
of King Alcinous is related by Homer in the central section of
the epic. It is placed in the mouth of the great adventurer,
who takes on himself a kind of "minstrelsy" ($\dot\rho\alpha\psi\omega\delta\acute\iota\alpha$), as he
words it, in order to offer the listening Phaeacians his real
story as a counterwork to the artful myth recited by De-
modocus. The storm begins to blow after the boats leave the
beach at Ismarus; for nine days the ruinous winds carry the
hero past Malea and Cythera to the Land of the Lotus-Eaters.
Even when the son of Hippotas gives the wanderers a wallet
containing the ways of the winds, a triumph of ill-counsel
brings the tempest again until further smash and bluster drive

[3] *Metamorphoses* XI.481–534.
[4] *Aeneid* I.81–141.
[5] *Bibliotheca* II.55–60.
[6] *Ibid.*, V.19–20. The same tale appears in the pseudo-Aristotle, *De
Mirabilibus Auscultationibus*, in *Opera*, ed. Bekker (Berlin, 1831), II, 836.

Odysseus with his single ship to the island of Circe. After she frees Odysseus and his companions and the dreaded rocks are avoided, the storms crash again, destroying all but the hero, who is carried after nine days to Ogygia "where dwelt Calypso of the braided hair." His release from this island at the request of the gods and his long and stormy voyage on the raft of his own making to the kingdom of Alcinous end the mighty story that he relates to the king and his white-armed wife, Arete. This is the way the topic begins: The hero crosses watery wastes impelled by power beyond his will; he arrives on islands or strands beyond the reach of the real; and there he finds a perfection of soul that makes actuality, when he returns to it, endurable. This is the ancient understanding of the travails of Odysseus, and it was not unknown to the Elizabethans. It seems possible to me that the story of Odysseus and its moral meaning may have colored for them the dramatic procedure of *The Tempest*.

To an Elizabethan who had the Greek and the stomach for the task, a number of commentaries explained the meaning that Homer hid beneath the literal fiction of Odysseus' wanderings in the islands. Armed with the popular notion that noble doctrine should be sugared with story, the Elizabethan might come to the labor of reading the Homeric commentaries of Heraclitus, Eustathius, Porphyrius, and the pseudo-Plutarch with more interest than these ancient exegetes can beget in us. The *De Vita et Poesi Homeri* of the pseudo-Plutarch argues that the Homeric poems are philosophical accounts of the physical nature of the world as well as ethical expositions of the vices and virtues.[7] Heraclitus demands that both epics be read as allegories. Only the ignorant, says he, who do not understand the language of allegory, who are incapable of recognizing truth, and who reject analogical interpretation, cling to the appearances of fiction. As a consequence, these

---

[7] Plutarch, *Opera*, ed. Dübner (Paris, 1875), V, 104.

ignoramuses are deaf to the voice of philosophy; but the wise, who hear the voice, go forward, accepting the *Iliad* and the *Odyssey* as guides to holy truth.[8] Some samples of this truth are apropos.

"All of the wanderings of Odysseus," writes Heraclitus, "if one regards them closely are great allegories. Homer invented this man in order to expound the nature of virtue and to serve the teaching of wisdom, because he detests the manifold vices that consume men."[9] The lotus is, consequently, a symbolic plant; it represents those pleasures and delights that cause men to forget their true home. The fact that Odysseus passes close to slaves of exotic and barbarian pleasures and is not tempted makes a shrewd moral point.[10] His temperance is further illustrated when he refuses, though starving, to eat the cattle of Helios. The temptations of Circe's island are obvious, but the reader must also understand that Hermes, who aids Odysseus in subduing the goddess, is a symbol, not a god in presence. Hermes is reason and dwells in Odysseus. When they seem to be talking, it is Odysseus reflecting or conversing with himself. The magic moly is the sign of reason; hence, it has black roots to represent the hard first steps in knowledge, but it terminates in a bright flower.[11] Such is the pagan reading; now we can continue this knotty explanation of Odysseus' wanderings by turning to Bishop Eustathius for the Christian message.

The island goddess Calypso, says Eustathius, is literally "the fair goddess," but she is also two abstract ideas. She is the body that confines the soul; and Odysseus, aided by Hermes-Reason, gives her up in order to return to Penelope, or Phi-

[8] *Quaestiones Homericae,* ed. Oelmann (Leipzig, 1910), p. 4.

[9] *Ibid.,* pp. 91–92.

[10] *Ibid.,* pp. 94–95.

[11] *Ibid.,* pp. 96–97; Alcinous is equated with the Epicurean philosophy; and hence, his kingdom has no charm for the Platonist Odysseus. Cf. pp. 105–106.

losophy. There is a second meaning. Calypso is the child (the thought) of Atlas, so she is clearly the science of astronomy and astrology. Odysseus, we know from other places in the epic, was well versed in starlore; but after Calypso has furthered his education in this science, he, realizing that it is only a minor branch of learning, returns to his wife, whose daily weaving and unweaving of her web shows that she is Philosophy.[12] So Eustathius finds moral readings here and in other episodes in the epic to support his conviction that the poem is a treatise on the education of men.[13]

There is no question that the sixteenth century saw these moral meanings in the stormblown ventures not only of Odysseus but also of his Latin reflection, Aeneas. When Chapman inscribed his translation of the *Odyssey* to the Earl of Somerset, he stated that a moral reading of the poem was a requirement. The *Iliad*, he writes, begins with the word "wrath," the *Odyssey* with "man"; the latter poem is, consequently, superior in moral instruction.

> In one, Predominant Perturbation; in the other, overruling Wisedome; in one, the Bodie's fervour and fashion of outward Fortitude to all possible height of Heroicall Action; in the other, the Mind's inward, constant and unconquerd Empire, unbroken, unaltered with any most insolent and tyrannous infliction. . . . Nor is this all-comprising Poesie phantastique, or meere fictive, but the most material and doctrinall illations of Truth, both for all manly information of Manners in the yong, all prescription of Justice, and even Christian pietie, in the most grave and high-governd. To illustrate both which in both kinds, with all height of expression, the Poet creates both a Bodie and a Soule in them—wherein, if the Bodie (being the letter, or historie) seemes fictive and beyond Possibilitie to bring into Act, the sence then and Allegorie (which is the Soule) is to be

[12] *Commentarii ad Homeri Odysseam* (Leipzig, 1825), I, 16–17
[13] *Ibid.*, II.4–5; Odysseus listens to the sirens because it is good for a philosopher to hear the poets.

sought—which intends a more eminent expressure of Vertue, for her lovelinesse, and of Vice, for her uglinesse, in their severall effects, going beyond the life than any Art within life can possibly delineate. Why then is Fiction to this end so hatefull to our true Ignorants? [14]

Heraclitus comes to life in the last sentence, but the tone of the whole passage implies that he was never really dead.

If Odysseus' journeys to the storm-set islands were allegories of the moral testing and education of men, we can, perhaps, assume that the voyage of Prospero and that of his enemies might have the same intent. We must notice at the start that the islands of the Greek epic and that of *The Tempest* are not exactly alike. The Greek islands are fantastic garden spots, direct mirrorings of the Isles of the Blest; they are not unlike the one that Diodorus' sailors found in the broad ocean. The Renaissance had not forgotten the Homeric islands, and we have only to turn to Ronsard's poem on Calypso to recapture their charm.

>   Terre grasse et fertille,
> Lieu que les Dieux avoient pour eux esleu,
> Pour tes forests autrefois tu m'as pleu,
> Pour tes jardins, pour tes belles fonteines,
> Et pour tes bords bien esmailles d'areines.[15]

Prospero's island, like Perdita's Arcadia, suffers intrusions from reality. In most instances we see the island through the eyes of Caliban, the only animal survivor now that its Circe (Sycorax) is dead. Through these banal eyes, we see that the island has fresh springs, brine pits, barren and fertile places, bogs, fens, flats. We learn through other eyes that there are desolate spots where there is "neither bush nor shrub." But it also has grassplots, "lush and lusty"; it produces berries,

[14] Homer, Chapman transl., ed. Nicoll (New York, 1956), II, 4–5.
[15] *Œuvres*, ed. Vaganay (Paris, 1924), IV, 218.

pignuts, crabapples, filberts, and limes. It is, however, no
thornless Eden, for—once again Caliban tells us—it has
"toothed briars, sharp furzes, pricking goss, and thorns."

When Prospero set foot on the island, it was not unlike
Circe's Aeaea, not honored "with a human shape." The blue-
eyed witch Sycorax (a true half-sister of the daughter of
Helios), whose antiquity is attested by her ability to "control
the moon," ruled the island with "earthy and abhorred com-
mands." The child of this earthy enchantress is naturally
earthy, an animal bent on animal pleasures, filled with animal
desires, haunted by animal fears. Odysseus broke the spell of
Circe; but Prospero, although he can undo the black magic of
Sycorax, is unable to raise Caliban to human estate. The island
has also some colors of Ogygia; but of Calypso, who sang with
sweet voice while she wove on her loom with a golden shuttle,
only the music and the knowledge are left. It is this music that
Ferdinand hears—the singing of the invisible Ariel—before
he sees Miranda, and so he speaks as Odysseus may have
spoken when, fresh from Hell and sea-peril, he saw the hu-
mane goddess "who took him in and treated him kindly."

> Most sure, the goddess
> On whom these airs attend. Vouchsafe my prayer
> May know if you remain upon this island,
> And that you will some good instruction give
> How I may bear me here.[16]

The music that diabolic magic imprisoned in a tree, heavenly
magic released, and now it has charms even for beast-hearted
men. "The isle is full of noises," says Caliban, "sound, and
sweet airs, that give delight and hurt not." [17] The two clowns,
made beasts by wine, "lifted up their noses/ As they smelt
music." [18] If in these respects the island has recollections of

---

[16] I.ii.420–25.
[17] III.ii.144–45.
[18] IV.i.177–78.

Ogygia, there are reminders of Calypso in both Prospero and Miranda: her wisdom in the father, her beauty in the girl. In Miranda there is a further quality of the Greek woman—the pity that only a goddess can have for men. "For I have a proper mind," says Calypso as she walks to the beach with Odysseus, "and my heart is not iron but as pitiful as yours." [19]

Prospero's island also brings to mind other literary islands of later date. Honorius, who wrote two thousand years after Homer, tells about the Island Perdita, charming, fertile, unknown to men. "Once you have found it by chance, if you leave it, you will never find it again." [20] This island like all lost islands—Atlantis, the island of the sybil who prophesied the birth of Christ, the islands of Delos unknown before the Flood—haunted the imagination of many generations. Sir John Mandeville knew many of these islands, and we can follow his sail from Crues to Lamary to Silha to the Isle of Bragman.[21] But the most popular legend which brought together saints, men of sin, and visions, is the story of Brendan, the Irish Odysseus, who found Island Perdita (lost by Honorius), the Island of Sheep (where the kine of the Sun are remembered), and the "Paradisus Avium" (where a great white tree was filled with Ariels).[22] He who has visited the islands of antiquity and of the Middle Ages has no difficulty in finding his way to those of the Renaissance.

When we visit the islands of the sixteenth century writers of romances, we sometimes find that they are also inhabited

[19] V.190–91.
[20] De Imago Mundi (PL, CLXXII, 132–33).
[21] The Travels, ed. Pollard (London, 1915), pp. 108–15, 119–39, 192–98.
[22] The Anglo-Norman Voyage of St. Brendan by Benedeit, ed. Waters (Oxford, 1928), pp. 23, 28–29; see also St. Brandan, ed. Wright (London, 1844); Sanct Brandan, ed. Schröder (Erlangen, 1871); Les voyages merveilleux de Saint Brandan, ed. Francisque-Michel (Paris, 1878); Die altfranzosische prosaübersetzung von Brendans Meerfahrt, ed. Wahlund (Upsala, 1900); An old Italian version of the Navigatio Sancti Brendani, ed. Waters (Oxford, 1931).

by women who stand in the ranks of magic between Sycorax and Circe. Ariosto's Alcina and Tasso's Armida are superb island enchantresses; but a better link between the experiences of Odysseus and Prospero is supplied by Francesco Bello's Mambrino, who sailed from France in fair weather and was overtaken by storm.

> Con sì gran furia allor mugghiava il mare,
> Che se il patron commanda non è inteso;
> Più non si può col timon governare,
> Col qual gran pezzo già s'era difeso
> Il cìel altro non fa che balenare;
> De la tempesta ognor duplica il peso,
> E sopra il legno in modo balzan l'onde,
> Che ognun in sè medesimo si confonde.[23]

Flung into the sea, Mambrino swims to the Isle of Monte Faggio, a place charming in palace and gardens and ruled by Carandina, who is described as a woman more gifted in magic than Zoroaster, Circe, and Medea. The hero and his companion, bewitched by her arts, live a luxurious life until they are reminded of their forgotten duties by a divine vision. This island miracle is suggestive but the experiences of Ariosto's Ruggiero are even more helpful for the moral interpretation of *The Tempest*.

The sea storm during which Ruggiero's conversion begins was mentioned in the last century as Shakespeare's literary model. This artistic relationship is probably untrue, but the career of the hero after the storm may enable us to add meaning to Shakespeare's play. Until he was swept into the sea, Ruggiero was a pagan; but as he swims, he remembers his unfulfilled vows and the loss of time. It occurs to him that he is being baptized in bitter salt water because he refused the sweet water of Christ's mercy. He makes a vow. By miracle,

[23] *Mambriano*, ed. Rua (Turin, 1926), I, 8.

"miracol fu," his swimming becomes easier and, like Prospero, he arrives at a providential island: "Nel solitario scoglio uscì Ruggiero, / Come all' alta Bontà divina piacque." Climbing a hill of juniper, laurel, myrtle, palm, and clear springs, he comes to the hermit's cell at the summit. Here the holy man greets him with the words that blind Saul heard on the Damascus road; [24] and Ruggiero's penitence, conversion, and religious education begin. These qualities of vision, conversion, penitence, and education—the archetypal influence of Patmos and the exiled St. John cannot be avoided—[25] attach themselves to the Christian island and may be transferred to the island that Shakespeare made in the Middle Sea.

The island of *The Tempest* is one in which pagan magic has been replaced by Christian miracle, and the maker of these miracles is a man who resembles to some degree an island saint. When we first encounter Prospero, he is "master of a full poor cell," not of the splendid palace surrounded by vast gardens of rare plants that once he may have possessed. The hermit who converted and instructed Ruggiero set fruit-bearing palms about his hut; and Prospero, equally modest, defends "this mouth o' the cell" with a grove of lime trees. In this

[24] *Orlando Furioso*, ed. Caretti (Milan-Naples, 1954), pp. 1061–64.
[25] Though Erasmus had questioned whether or not St. John the Apostle was also the writer of the Book of The Revelation and was followed in this position by Sebastian Castellio, who called him "Joannes Theologus" as did some of the Fathers (see his *Biblia* [Basel, 1565], p. 486), the post-Trent Vulgate and the Protestant scholars thought of the two Johns as one man. The nature of their arguments is summed up by Beza in the prolegomena to the Apocalypse in the *Biblia* (Hanover, 1602). The usual legend read that John was exiled to Patmos by Diocletian and there not only preached the faith but had his vision: see J. Camerarius, *Historia Jesu Christi . . . Itemque de Apostolis* (Leipzig, 1581), p. 124; and Surius, *De Probatis Sanctorum Historiis* (Cologne, 1575), VI, 1013. The notion of an island saint is not too uncommon. In *Le Roman en Prose de Tristan* (ed. Löseth [Paris, 1890]), Sadoc is thrown overboard during a storm and swims to some rocks where he is saved by an eremite and where he lives for three years (pp. 4–5).

place, the banished Duke lives and meditates; there are even periods when he shuts himself off, like an anchorite, from all human conversation. But this is credible because Prospero was something of an eremite before his scheming, worldly brother deprived him of the dukedom:

> I thus neglecting worldly ends, all dedicate
> To closeness, and the bettering of my mind.[26]

"Closeness" is a word that explains the Prospero whom we know; he is an aloof man, who stands apart or rises above (as if he were a playwright) the other characters in the drama that his secret powers have made.

On Shakespeare's lost island, Prospero was first his daughter's schoolmaster; it is here that she had her only education.

> Here in this island we arrived, and here
> Have I, thy schoolmaster, made thee more profit
> Than other princess can, that have more time
> For vainer hours, and tutors not so careful.[27]

The admirable and sympathetic Miranda has attempted, in turn, to teach Caliban the Italian language; but her lessons have been partially wasted, because, like so many poor linguists, the man-brute has only an ear for profanity. Prospero, too, has tried unsuccessfully to give lessons to the son of Sycorax. But while he was teaching others, Prospero taught himself, learning, first, about his own nature and, next, how to predict and control his inner weather. In this control, he surpasses his old foe Alonso, who is "cloudy" over the loss of Ferdinand until he, too, is educated by the man he helped to depose. There are occasions when the lightning still flashes in the sky of Prospero's anger, but he never inflicts, as he was quite able to do, another tempest on his storm-driven enemies.

[26] I.ii.89–90
[27] I.ii.171–74.

> Though with their high wrongs I am stuck to th' quick,
> Yet, with my nobler reason 'gainst my fury
> Do I take part. The rarer action is
> In virtue than in vengeance. They being penitent,
> The sole drift of my purpose doth extend
> Not a frown further.[28]

Though education is preliminary to conversion, it is only a preparative requirement, and Prospero, whose real change of heart may have begun when his raft reached the island, knows about that process, too.

Before the hapless wedding party arrived on the island—we should notice the difference between Prospero and Alonso as matchmakers—Prospero tried to dissuade Caliban from the worship of Setebos; but it is useless to attempt the conversion of those who are guided by the lowest levels of the soul.

> A devil, a born devil, on whose nature
> Nurture can never stick; on whom my pains,
> Humanely taken, all, all lost, quite lost,
> And as with age his body uglier grows,
> So his mind cankers.[29]

With the newcomers his task is easier, because they are supposedly Christians from a Christian land. Actually, only Gonzalo is a real Christian, who testifies to his faith on all occasions. He joins the King in prayers; he believes in "the miracle" of preservation; he comforts the suffering King; he plans, to the amusement of the scoffers, a Christian state; he trusts heaven; he calls on "the name of something holy"; he requests the guidance of "some heavenly power"; he asks the gods "to look down"; and his last speech in the play is "Be it so, Amen." There is plain piety in almost every word he utters, and everything he does explains his earlier act of dangerous charity to Prospero and the infant Miranda. Gonzalo has grace enough

[28] V.i.25–30.
[29] IV.i.188–92.

for sainthood, but he is associated with men whose need for spiritual rehabilitation is obvious.

The clowns, Trinculo and Stephano, are almost too stupid for salvation. They will run down the primrose path to the eternal bonfire, forever boisterous, forever drunk, forever singing the libertine's song: "Flout 'em and scout 'em, and scout 'em and flout 'em; / Thought is free!" Paired with them are the freethinking and worldly cynics, Sebastian and Antonio. The atheism of Antonio is made clear when he is asked, after proposing murder, about the state of his conscience.

> But I feel not
> This deity in my bosom. Twenty consciences
> That stand 'twixt me and Milan, candied be they,
> And melt ere they molest.[30]

It is only by a kind of angelic intervention through the miracle of music that the crime of murder is avoided. Conscience finally comes to Antonio as it does to the other "men of sin," and it comes, as we might expect, because of the nature of islands, through a vision. In this case the vision is that of a banquet served by mysterious ministers. With the appearance of these harmonious servants, the doubting sinners begin to believe. Religious words fill the mouth of Alonso; the sceptical Sebastian and Antonio, smitten dumb by the spectacle, find their tongues with the word "believe." Gonzalo, true to his pious nature, thinks that he sees the realization of his Christian community, that he has arrived on Mandeville's Island of Bragman.

> For certes these are people of the island—
> Who, though they are of monstrous shape, yet note,
> Their manners are more gentle-kind than of
> Our human generation you shall find
> Many, nay, almost any.[31]

[30] II.i.277–80
[31] III.iii.30–34.

Then, as speculation gives way to hunger, Ariel appears in the form of a harpy and the banquet vanishes like a dream. To understand Ariel's appearance as a harpy and the nature of the banquet, we must go, as Shakespearean annotators have gone, to the third book of the *Aeneid;* but we must apply the speech of Celaeno, as it has not been applied, to the lecture of Ariel. "I, the eldest of the Furies," says the harpy Celaeno, "reveal it to you." "Vobis Furiarum ego maxima pando." [32] Harpies are Furies; they both bring divine vengeance. Valerius Flaccus affirms the testimony of Vergil when he writes that the harpies thrust the earned anger of the gods on men.[33] But harpies are more than this. Hesiod says that they are "beautiful creatures of the wind and air";[34] whereas Homer, who does not mention their beauty, identifies them with "the spirits of the storm." In the fourteenth book of the *Odyssey,* Eumaeus gives us a key text: "νῦν δέ μιν ἀκλεεῶς ἄρέπυιαι ἀνηρείψαντο" (371). So Ariel, the beautiful spirit of the air, who made the storm of the first scene, is also a Harpy-Fury who troubles the minds of the three sinners. "Holy" Gonzalo, who observes the change in the countenance and manner of the three, cannot withhold his observation: "Their great guilt . . . 'gins to bite the spirits." The effect of the lecture of Conscience is greater than biting; Antonio and Sebastian, who thought they had the power in pocket, twist in its mighty grasp.

> Thou art pinched for't now Sebastian. Flesh and blood,
> You brother mine, that entertained ambition,
> Expelled remorse and nature, who, with Sebastian—
> Whose inward pinches therefore are most strong—
> Would here have killed your King.[35]

[32] III.252.
[33] IV.428–61.
[34] *Theogonia* 265.
[35] V.i.74–78.

Faithful to tradition, the island of education, saints, and visions, is also a place of repentance and conversion; but the visions do not end with one that produces a change of heart.

For the troth-plight of his daughter and Ferdinand, Prospero makes a pleasant, yet visionary, masque of spirits who are borrowed, except for the realistic British harvestmen, from the mythological records. To point the difference between the two kinds of visions, Shakespeare makes Ferdinand say in the middle of the second:

> This is a most majestic vision, and
> Harmonious charmingly. May I be bold
> To think these spirits? [36]

Prospero admits that they are spirits, whom he has called forth to act his "present fancies." His fancies are worth noticing because they reveal the ultimate Shakespearean resolution of the fate of man. The theme of the masque is fertility in marriage, a theme annotated for us by Ferdinand's vow of prenuptial chastity. Such a condition is impossible for Caliban, the rapist, and his new-found human gods; they accept propagation, but sacraments are not for them. Because their sort of love is excluded from the idealism of the island, Venus and her son are omitted from Prospero's cast of characters. Iris informs us that the heroine of *Venus and Adonis* has departed with her son for Paphos.

> Here thought they to have done
> Some wanton charm upon this man and maid,
> Whose vows are, that no bed-right shall be paid
> Till Hymen's torch be lighted.[37]

So the goddess of marriage, Juno, and the goddess of fertility, Ceres, are the principal actors in this blessed vision, which concludes with the symbolic August scene of harvest and gar-

[36] IV.i.118–20.
[37] IV.i.94–97.

ner. The masque, it must be noticed, is structurally bound to the play through the character of Iris, who, in her mythological guises, is the messenger of the goddesses, a virgin,[38] and, better still, sister to the Harpies.[39] It is a part that Ariel could and did play with great skill.

The masque is one of the dramatic centers of the play, and in its simple theme of immortality through generation we have again the doctrine that lighted most of Shakespeare's days on earth. Though I shall return to this, I want first—now that the island is for the moment so plainly a place of vision—to ponder the secondary emphasis in this play, as in previous ones, on the world of vision and dream. This emphasis is finely stated when Prospero speaks his famous lines concluding the revels.

> These our actors,
> As I foretold you, were all spirits, and
> Are melted into air, into thin air;
> And like the baseless fabric of this vision,
> The cloud-capped towers, the gorgeous palaces,
> The solemn temples, the great globe itself,
> Yea all which it inherit, shall dissolve,
> And like this insubstantial pageant faded
> Leave not a rack behind. We are such stuff
> As dreams are made on; and our little life
> Is rounded with a sleep.[40]

Within the boundaries of this utterance, Shakespeare accepts the philosophy of mortal existence against which the dark plays protest. Because once again he accepts the promise of the masque, the benediction of Juno and the rewards of Ceres, he can also accept the necessary condition that men and their works, as he knew them, are only visions and will dissolve like summer clouds. If the world that each man has made is a

[38] Theocritus, *Eidyllion* XVII.134; Vergil, *Aeneid* V.610.
[39] Hesiod, *op. cit.*, 266, 780.
[40] IV.i.146–57.

vision, then life as each man possesses it is a dream. To expound this idea, sturdy tradition aids us mortals, who like Christopher Sly have only "an after-dinner's sleep" between youth and age, to comprehend the topics that Prospero's aria reveals.

First, it is interesting to scrutinize the dream metaphors in *The Tempest*. Miranda, mindful of her childhood, says that it was "rather like a dream than an assurance"; and Ferdinand, under the spell of both the girl and her father, finds his "spirits" all bound up "as in a dream." The Boatswain, no philosopher, thinks of dreams when he searches his mind for a figure to express the rapid course of time: "On a trice, so please you, / Even in a dream, were we divided from them." Even Caliban, earth and filth that he is, brings dream and music together to describe the island:

> and then, in dreaming,
> The clouds methought would open, and show riches
> Ready to drop upon me, that when I waked
> I cried to dream again.[41]

Throughout Shakespeare's plays—and the custom is not peculiar to him alone—*dream* is a metaphor of *life*, as if it were difficult to separate the life of dreams from conscious existence.

The origin of this imagistic comparison begins, I suppose, with human time. The Gentile hero, Job, whose poet almost got him canonized, says of the lot of man: "He shall fly away as a dream, and shall not be found: yea, he shall be chased away as a vision of night." [42] Across the lines of Jehovah's territory were less consecrated poets who would agree. For Pindar, "man is a shadow's dream." [43] and Sophocles describes men in the *Ajax* as "dreams or shadows." [44] Aristophanes sum-

---

[41] III.ii.149–52.
[42] Job 20:8.
[43] *Pyth*.8.95–96.
[44] 126.

mons men, who "pass like dreams of sorrow," to listen to the
singing of the *Birds*.[45] The Middle Ages improved on these
images of the Greeks and the Romans to such an extent that its
child and reformer, the optimistic Petrarch, could complain
about the dreamlike quality of existence. He writes to Gia-
como Colonna that life is a dream or shifting fancy. "Illa
relegenti, totam mihi vitam meam, nihil videri aliud quam leve
somnium, fugacissimumque phantasma." [46] It is interesting that
this passage comes from a letter on the subject of the vanished
glories of Rome, a city that had long been the subject of medi-
tations on the transitoriness of mortal achievement.

Prospero's reverie about "cloud-capped towers," "gorgeous
palaces," and "solemn temples" is a metropolitan intrusion
into the primitive island realm. The former duke remembers
the land across the waters, the cities of Carthage or of the
Italian mainland. "The great globe itself" may be a playful
allusion to the theater on the Bankside, and the whole speech
may wave away the theatrical world of painted cloth and
tinsel; but this is not a speech to father laughter or even smiles,
for its conclusion is grave and its total import is serious. Man
passes and so does what he makes. "My weakness . . . my old
brain . . . my infirmity . . . my beating mind." The mind
of the Renaissance reader is directed by Prospero's words not
to the island or to England, but to Rome, the ruined imperial
city, where man had pondered for many generations on the
impermanence of life and art.[47]

[45] 686–87.

[46] *Opera* (Basel, 1554), p. 667.

[47] There was present in the imperial Romans, who looked on the ruins
of Athens ("vacuae Athenae," says Horace in *Epistulae* II.2.81), a modest
sense of personal unworthiness and the melting glory of man; nonetheless,
they were equally possessed by a reassurance that man's material remainders
contain and preserve him. An anonymous late Latin poet might write a
poignant epitaph of the great city in which the autumnal music of the
Middle Ages is audible (*Anthologia Latina*, ed. Riese [Leipzig, 1922],
I, 267), yet the view of the mighty city stirred emotions far more deep.

The Middle Ages had two opinions about the fallen towers, palaces, and temples of Rome. One was that the material ruin that lay about the sojourner in the city was full evidence of its spiritual ruin.[48] Alcuin saw in the broken stones the great symbol of the foolishness of human glory. "Roma, caput mundi, mundi decus, aurea Roma / Hunc remanet tantum saeva ruina tibi." [49] To a second group, of which Hildebert of Lavardin [50] is a good representative, there are two Romes: the ruined center of paganism and the splendid capital city of the Christian world. For Dante the ruins are venerable; [51] and though Petrarch reads their lesson, he hopes to see splendor reborn from the debris that by itself filled him with adoration.[52] Some of the humanists agreed with the mediaeval sermons on the ruins, but most of them saw in the fallen arches and columns the fragility of all human effort. Poggio finds dignity and greatness in the

---

Propertius escapes from the obdurate Cynthia to *doctae Athenae* to purge himself of foul passions by seeing those places in which were stored recollections of noble emotions and of men healed of error (III.21.25–30). Cicero describes a walk among its ruins that, he says, made the persons of Sophocles, Plato, and Epicurus more vivid to him than their books (*De Finibus* V.1–6). Two centuries later, Dio Chrysostom pondered the ruined land, but he was certain that the ruins make manifest the greatness of Greece (*Orationes* VII.38–39) for the ruins are far more gracious than the living cities (XXXI.160).

[48] "Versus Romae," in *Poetae Latini Aevi Carolini*, ed. Traube (Berlin, 1896), III, 555–56. This poem is discussed by A. Graf, *Roma nella Memoria e nelle Immaginazioni del Medio Evo* (Turin, 1882), I, 46–47. This pioneer work has been somewhat superseded by Schneider, *Rom und Romedanke im Mittelalter* (Munich, 1926), but it is still the best for literary texts.

[49] *Opera*, ed. Dümmler (Berlin, 1891), I, 230.

[50] B. Haureau, *Notices et Extraits des Quelques Manuscrits Latins de la Bibliothèque Nationale* (Paris, 1890–1893), pp. 330–36. The theme appears in Sedulius Scottus, *Carmina*, ed. Traube, *PLAC* (Berlin, 1896) III, 170–76; in a tenth-century poem in Novati, *L'Influsso del Pensiero Latino* (Milan, 1899), pp. 172–74; and in Neckham, *De Laudibus Divinae Sapientiae*, ed. Wright (London, 1863), p. 445.

[51] There have been numerous studies of Dante's attitude; for the most recent, see Davis, *Dante and the Idea of Rome* (Oxford, 1957).

[52] *Opera* (Basel, 1554), pp. 731, 1169.

ruin—"sola ruina praeteritam dignitatem ac magnitudinem ostentantem"—but he is also moved by them to speculate on the power of Fortuna, a non-Christian lady.[53] Traversari reads them as torn documents, to the same end,[54] and Urceus wanders through the decaying city to write an epigram on man's fate.

> Roma fuit periere patres periere quirites
> Restat deserto sola ruina solo
> Quaeque tamen restat doctorum poena virorum
> Hic labor; hic non sunt praemia: nulla quies.[55]

The poets of the vernacular follow the same themes, and the ruins, as symbols of man's tender hold on life and the world, haunt such lyrics as Castiglione's "Superbi colli, e voi sacre ruine," and Guidicconi's "Degna nutrice de le chiare genti." The sixteenth-century Italian poet, Bernardino Baldi, who wrote a sonnet sequence on Rome, likewise saw in the wreckage about him the eternal lesson of the "insubstantial pageant faded." A fragment of his poem on the Coliseum is sample enough of the mode and mood.

> Da questo campo abbandonato ed ermo,
> Cui fanno alte ruine ampia corona,
> Prender può esempio ogni mortal persona
> Come contro l'eta perda ogni schermo.
> O fugaci bellezze, o mondo infermo,
> O nostra fama che sì breve suona,
> Ben sei nubilo ciel che splende e tuona
> Tutto in un punto, e nulla è 'n te di fermo.[56]

Although the Italian poets lamented the ruins of Rome, they also lived on them. The distance was not great enough for real

---

[53] *De Fortunae . . . Romae et de Ruina Eiusdem*, in De Sallengre, *Novus Thesaurus* (Hague, 1716), I, 502.

[54] Graf, *op. cit.*, I, 52.

[55] *Silvae* (Venice, 1506), Li verso.

[56] *Versi e Prose*, ed. Ugolini and Polidori (Florence, 1859), p. 258.

nostalgia. It was a French poet, Du Bellay, who built these broken stones into a giant European symbol of evanescence. In the sonnets of *Les Antiquitez* and in the Latin "Romae Descriptio," Du Bellay proclaimed his love of the past and told his contemporaries what their future contained. These sonnets are separate and numbered, but they seem like stanzas in a long poem on the inconstant nature of life. In some the poet imitates Latin and Italian predecessors; in others he makes poetic excursions into history; but there is always the implication of decay, the sense of impermanence. Rome may seem to be renewing herself, but we may look at her broken body for the mortal lesson (XXVII). She resists time, but time will have her in the end (VII). Only the flowing Tiber is unchanged because only change endures in a world of change (III). Consolation is to be found, but it is the consolation of mutability.

> Ainsi quand du grand Tout le fuite retournée,
> Ou trentesix mil' ans ont sa course bornée,
> Rompra des elemens le naturel accord,
> Les semences qui sont meres de toutes choses,
> Retourneront encor' a leur premier discord,
> Au ventre du Chaos eternellement closes. (XXI)

When Prospero talks about ruined towers, temples, and palaces, he may be speaking in general terms, but a travelled Jacobean who listened to him would certainly think of the waste of Imperial Rome. No dream was ever greater than this imperial one; no dream ever passed more sadly and left grander evidence of its passing. The text for Prospero's speech was provided by *Lear:* "Oh ruined piece of nature; this great world / Shall so wear out to naught." But a world and a life that are dreams is a common enough theme for Shakespeare. The fate of the dreamer is a great topic in all the tragedies, whose heroes, dreams in themselves, awaken from dreams unable to endure the reality in which they find themselves. The island is where they were born, and when they cross to the mainland, they learn that they "are the stuff that dreams are made on." With *The Tempest* Shakespeare returns to his old belief in the continuity of man—the heroes of the tragedies, even Lear, die childless. The doctrine is a simple one. Life will go on; only the individual passes. This is the "brave new world."

CHAPTER FOUR

George Herbert

"The Rose"

The poetry of George Herbert, like that of Henry Vaughan, is mainly supported by the metaphoric tradition of the Bible and the Liturgy. For this reason its images should not be difficult for the reader who has lived in a Christian community. But although the allusions are not necessarily clear, Herbert does not really intend to trap us. He simply assumes that as Christians we have Christian knowledge. When he put aside his vast classical learning (plain enough in his Latin and Greek verse), when he abandoned the "dark style" and burned his papers, he almost dismissed the searcher for hidden symbolism from his company:

> Must all be vail'd, while he that reades, divines,
> Catching the sense at two removes.

In spite of Herbert's conscious pursuit of plainness and lucidity, there are occasions when a knowledge of the traditions, known to him but now strange to us, brushes away difficulty, or, as in the case of "The Rose," expounds the classical and Christian symbols of the poem and enhances its meaning.

The most familiar rose poem of the seventeenth century is not that of Herbert, but Herrick's revision of Ausonius' "Collige rosas," which gathers into its four stanzas the full sadness of transitoriness as it is expressed by the fragility of flowers, the rising and setting of the suns, and the winged departure of youth. These definitions of the rose are traditional, and Herrick does little more than turn their classical past into an English present. The same topic returns with somewhat more suavity and a finer meaning in Waller's "Go, Lovely Rose"; but this poem, too, pleasant as it is, maintains the pagan and hence worldly transcription of the flower as a sign of human hopelessness and helplessness. It is Herbert's poem, conscious of the worldly tradition, that brings in the Christian meanings of the flower and permits the pagan rose to be contrasted with the spiritual one. The text of the poem should now lie before us.

> Presse me not to take more pleasure
>   In this world of sugred lies,
> And to use a larger measure
>   Then my strict, yet welcome size.
>
> First, there is no pleasure here:
>   Colour'd griefs indeed there are,
> Blushing woes, that look as cleare
>   As if they could beautie spare.
>
> Or if such deceits there be,
>   Such delights I meant to say;
> There are no such things to me
>   Who have pass'd my right away.
>
> But I will not much oppose
>   Unto what you now advise:

Onely take this gentle rose,
     And therein my answer lies.

What is fairer then a rose?
     What is sweeter? yet it purgeth.
Purgings enmitie disclose,
     Enmities forbearance urgeth.

If then all that worldlings prize
     Be contracted to a rose;
Sweetly there indeed it lies,
     But it biteth in the close.

So this flower doth judge and sentence
     Worldly joyes to be a scourge:
For they all produce repentance,
     And repentance is a purge.

But I health, not physick choose:
     Onely though I you oppose,
Say that fairly I refuse,
     For my answer is a rose.

It is possible that the meaning of this poem would be reasonably clear to someone who did not know the symbolic history of the rose. An uninformed reader would discover that the first four stanzas summarize the advice given the poet by a child of the world; whereas the latter four stanzas are the poet's replies based on the lesson of the rose. "Onely take this gentle rose,/ And therein my answer lies." The first four stanzas do not seem to be about the rose, but it is quite plain that the flower, symbolically unfolded petal by petal in the second part of the poem, is substantially present in the first. The opening lines, "Presse me not to take more pleasure/ In this world of sugred lies" has two literal meanings. The man of the world has urged Herbert to take more pleasure in material things, but the rose is also pressed to make an electuary called "sugar of roses." When we notice this second meaning, we also see that the rose as well as the poet is a speaker in the first stanzas, and we shall learn from tradition that the lecture on the rose in the second part is delivered by a man and a rose. The double nature of the rose is the subject of continuous poetic comment. The flower is fair and sweet, but it purges. The purge discloses the cause of the malady and indicates where temperance is required. Or we can read this in another fashion. Lying in the hand, the rose is sweet; close the fist on it and discover its thorns. This is the life of the world, sweet in the opening but bitter in the close, leading to final purgation or repentance, to eventual judgment and sentence. Since the poet does not wish to be made sick with worldliness, his answer is "a rose." To see all of these meanings, we need only read; but a knowledge of the metaphoric tradition of roses makes these observations firmer and more elegant.

The rose is a metaphor of worldliness in poems of antiquity, and it is a worldliness that passes swiftly. The flower is bright in the crown of Eros, as we discover when Anacreon puts it into verse:

'Ρόδον ὦ παῖς ὁ κυθήρης
Στέφεται καλοὺς ἰούλους,
Χαρίτεσσι συγχορεύων. . . . ,[1]

Yet the blossom that is here fresh will not last, for neither roses nor love, says Philostratus, endure: "χρόνον δ' οὔτ Ἔρως οὔτε ῥόδα οἶδεν."[2] The same theme of transient loveliness is sorrowfully echoed by Horace, "Nimium breves/ Flores amoenae ferre jube rosae";[3] and if we turn to Ovid, we are reminded of the short existence of beauty in terms of the rose.

Forma bonum fragile est; quantumque accedit ad annos
Fit minor; et spatio carpitur ipsa suo.

[1] XLIV.9–11.
[2] *Epistolae* LV.34.
[3] *Carmina* II.3.13–14

Nec violae semper, nec hiantia lilia florent;
Et riget amissa spina relicta rosa.[4]

The flower that stood for love, and youth, and the brevity of both continued to bloom throughout the Middle Ages in gardens where Venus and her child conversed and lovers came for their benediction. In such a garden grew the "grant Rosier" of the *Romance of the Rose,* and the renowned lovers, Florance and Blanche Flor, support this symbolism when they make rendezvous on a May morning in a place where "Roses i ot entremellées/ Les lates i sont bien ovrées."[5]

During the Renaissance the rose poem of Anacreon was rendered into French by Belleau,[6] and other members of the *Pléiade* knew the flower in all of its symbolic transformations. Ronsard begins one of his sonnets to Marie with the metaphor of the rose, sacred to Venus but brief as a perfume.

Douce, belle, amoureuse et bien fleurente Rose,
Que tu es à bon droit a amours consacrée;
Ta delicate odeur hommes et Dieux recrée,
Et bref, Rose, tu es belle sur toute chose.[7]

The rose is consecrated to love and love's little moment, and owing to a theme of Catullus[8] that Ariosto[9] enlarged, the flower was used to celebrate a love of a virginal sort.

La vierge est semblable à la rose
Qui fleurist dans un beau jardin,
Sur l'espineux rosier declose:
Elle a la rosee au matin:
La terre, l'eau, l'air, le vent doux,
Qui leur faveur luy donnent tous.[10]

[4] *Ars* II.113–16.
[5] *Fablieux et Contes,* ed. Barbazon (Paris, 1807), IV, 360.
[6] *Œuvres* I.43.
[7] *Œuvres,* ed. Marty-Laveaux (Paris, 1924), II, 22.
[8] LXII.39–47.
[9] *Orlando Furioso* I.42–43.
[10] Baif, *Œuvres* I.295. See DuBellay, *L'Olive* XCVII.

Baif who wrote this can, in his elaborate "Les Roses," com-
ment at length on the Ausonian theme; but it is the master,
Ronsard, who condenses all the topics and sweeps the way for
Herrick.

Mignonne, allons voir si la rose
Qui ce matin avoit declose
Sa robe de pourpre au Soleil,
A point perdu cette vesprée,
Les plis de sa robe pourprée
Et son teint au vostre pareil.
Las! voyez comme en peu d'espace,
Mignonne, elle a dessus la place
Las, las, ses beautez laissé cheoir!
O vrayment marastre Nature,
Puis qu'une telle fleur ne dure
Que du matin jusques au soir.
Donc, si vous me croyez, mignonne,
Tandis que votre âge fleuronne
En sa plus verte nouveauté,
Cueillez, cueillez vostre jeunesse:
Comme à ceste fleur la vieillesse
Fera ternir vostre beauté.[11]

So with this group of French poets, the rose retains its ancient
values; it is the sign of love, of young virgins, of ephemerality,
and even of death;[12] but the flower had other meanings than
these.

Although the rose made the chaplet of Venus and wreathed
the sickle of Chronos, the ancients also wove it into the crowns
of the disciples of Bacchus. In its vinous connection the rose
had a double sense, for it not only adorned the brows of the
wine-god but reminded the rose-crowned revellers of the sick
tribulations of the next morning. Philostratus, consequently,

[11] *Op. cit.*, III.75–76.
[12] See Ronsard, "Ode a Monsieur d'Orleans" III.163; "Sur la mort de
Marie" II.22.

describes Comus with a disorderly crown of roses slipping from his drunken head; [13] and Propertius [14] and Martial associate the flower with alcoholic relaxation. The latter poet, sending some verses to Pliny, advises the Muse who will be his messenger to seek out that learned and diligent man after sundown, when roses reign with the wine-god.

> Seras tutior ibis ad lucernas:
> Haec hora est tua, cum furit Lyaeus,
> Cum regnat rosa, cum madent capilli:
> Tunc me vel rigidi legant Catones.[15]

To make all of this plainer, Ovid describes an evening when Bacchus came with roses, with Flora and her daughters. Flora, he tells us, is not one of those sour ones, "not one of those high nosed ones"; "she advises us by a vision of age to use life while it flowers; the thorn is despised after the rose falls." "Et monet aetatis specie, dum floreat, uti;/ Contemni spinam, cecidere rosae." [16] This is, of course, the rosy path, the world through rose-colored glasses, "the colored griefs," "the blushing woes." We stagger through a riot of antique roses to hear the Comus of Milton sing "ad lucernas":

> Braid your Locks with rosy Twine
> Dropping odours, dropping Wine.
> Rigour now is gone to bed,
> And advice with scrupulous head
> Strict Age, and sour Severity,
> With their grave Saws in slumber lie.

In the sour dawn, let us hear "sour Severity."

"The Christian," Tertullian states, "will not wear a crown of flowers." [17] This prohibition is strongly supported by

---

[13] *Imagines* I.2.4.
[14] III.5.21–22.
[15] X.19.19–21.
[16] *Fasti* V.335–54.
[17] *Opera,* ed. Kroymann (Vienna, 1942), II, 2, p. 156.

Clement of Alexandria when he writes about crowns: crowns
of flowers and floral perfumes are not needed by Christians;
the banqueting room and the scent-house are not for them.
"To us, who are not only forbidden drunkenness but also the
liberal use of wine, crowns of roses and violets are of no
use." [18] Prudentius, master of Christian verse, places all of this
before us when he commends the man who can sit to supper
without a crown of flowers or perfumes.

> Hic mihi nulla rosae spolia,
> Nullus aromate fragrat odor,
> Sed liquor influit ambrosius,
> Nectareamque fidem redolet.[19]

This Christian is not unlike Prudentius' St. Eulalia, who
scorned "the roses of the world" in order to win her "crown
of life." [20] So after a few centuries of Christian striving, the
rose as the sign of wine and riot, of Bacchus and Venus, has
lost its fragrance and its beauty; it stands, as Herbert says, for
the "deceits" of life. But as we notice this, we also remember
the last great symbol of the *Divina Commedia*, the "candida
rosa"; and we know, too, that the Mother of God is the rose
without a thorn. The rose which stood for virgins and fleshly
love has come to be the sign of the Virgin and heavenly love.

St. Ambrose was, I think, the first gardener to discover the
rose, thornless indeed, in the landscape of an Eden through
which the first human pair wandered.[21] Dracontius, who knew
his classical poets well enough to describe in his "De Origine
Rosarum," as Herrick does, how roses first "came red," notices
the flower, too, as he follows Adam and Eve through the garden. "They walked through flowers and gardens all of roses."

[18] *Opera*, ed. Dindorff (Oxford, 1869), I, 267, 276.
[19] *Carmina*, ed. Dressel (Leipzig, 1860), pp. 14–15.
[20] "Spernere sucina, flare rosas, /Fulva monilia respuere," *ibid.*, pp. 332–33.
[21] *Opera*, ed. Schenkl (Vienna, 1897), I, 91.

"Ibant per flores et tota rosaria laeti." [22] St. Avitus, the first Christian poet of France, looks at the Adamic plantation with the eye of a flower lover.

> Lilia perlucent nullo flaccentia sole
> Nec tactus violat violas roseumque ruborem
> Servans perpetuo suffundit gratia vultu.[23]

Once the scene of man's fall is ablaze with roses, the flower, denied to the temperate Christian as a crown, becomes a sign of conjugal love. When Milton describes Adam and Eve embracing and asleep while "the flow'ry roof/ Show'r'd Roses, which the Morn repair'd," he is reminding us that the rose had something to do with love on a sacramental level; [24] and after proper consultation with St. Ambrose, the English poet tells us that these roses are "without thorn." [25] We are thus ready to understand why Eve, the thorn in man's flesh, is replaced by Mary, the rose on the thornless bush.

The roses that flourished in the good soil of the earthly paradise were brought thither from Heaven, for Milton informs us that the bright floor of God's land was "Impurpl'd with Celestial Roses." [26] Milton did not invent this fact because Prudentius, who denied crowns of earthly roses to Christians, describes the roses of the celestial fields: "Illic purpureis tecta rosariis/ Omnis fragrat humus." [27] A few generations later, Venantius Fortunatus wrote a poem about Heaven and the spiritual virgins, as he calls them, wandering through its meadows as they gather heavenly roses and violets.[28] These blessed ones wear triple crowns, feed their eyes

---

[22] *Carmina*, ed. Vollmer (Berlin, 1905), p. 46.
[23] *Opera*, ed. Peiper (Berlin, 1883), p. 209.
[24] *Paradise Lost* IV.772–73.
[25] *Ibid.*, 256.
[26] *Ibid.*, III.364.
[27] *Op. cit.*, p. 31.
[28] *Opera*, ed. Leo (Berlin, 1881), p. 182.

on roses and lilies, and breathe the divine perfumes. "Floribus aeternis oculos rosa lilia pascunt/ Et paradisiacus naribus intrat odor." [29] The crowns and perfumes denied to Christians on earth are eternally theirs in Heaven.

So the rose of love and virginity, covering the floor of Heaven and decorating the Garden, is also a part of the Christian botany. Dante finds it in his sky and makes it into a purer and higher sign—at its heart the bees of Christ drink nectar. The rose has spiritual grace; the rose has moral significance. The virgins of Fortunatus are not to be confused with those of that almost-persuaded pagan, Ausonius, and the spiritualized flower is to be understood as a sign of virginal modesty. In a letter to Rusticus, who should know the flower, St. Jerome describes it as a superior instructress in modesty.[30] Alexander Neckham, who probably listened to some of the secular rose songs of the *Carmina Burana*, writes a little poem about the virginity of roses and their medicinal uses, showing that the flower, like all important symbols, has many meanings simultaneously.

> Et rosa, purpureo vestita rubore decenter
> Vernans est horti gloria, laetus honos.
> Flos est virginibus aptus, gratusque juventae,
> Grataque virginei signa pudoris habet.
> Virginis est speculum rosa vernans, sed cito marcens,
> Et quod sit species res fugitiva docet.[31]

But blushes of virgins are no more red than the blood of martyrs, and the rose, fragile flower that it was, could accept that symbolic burden, too.

The legends of the martyrs, we remember, are garlanded with roses. St. Dorothea says to the proconsul, who gives her a choice of idolatry or death, "I am ready to suffer as you desire and I shall do it for Jesus Christ, my spouse, with whom

---

[29] *Ibid.*, p. 192.
[30] *Epistolae*, ed. Hilberg (Vienna, 1918), p. 120.
[31] *De Laudibus Divinae Sapientiae*, ed. Wright (London, 1863), p. 479.

I shall have eternal life. I have gathered roses, spices, and fruit in his delicious garden."[32] St. Rose of Lima, according to the *Acta Sanctorum*, gathered roses in the garden and threw them into the air as an offering to the "Great Gardener." The flowers hung in the sky, then formed themselves into a cross, the rosy-cross, symbol of their acceptability to Christ.[33] Besides the legends, the poetry of martyrology is adorned with rose metaphors. Sometimes the saints shine in their crowns of roses;[34] sometimes the rose itself awards a garland to a dying Christian.[35] The rose, pagan sign of worldly pleasure, is also the emblem of those who scorn the world and its fragile joys. The martyr, who seeks for everlasting life, becomes in this world the ephemeral rose.

The equation between roses and Christians can be further extended, for the rose represented any Christian who lived in the thorn patch of the flesh. St. Ambrose writes that the rose, once it has taken thorns, is the symbol of man surrounded by the briars of pricking care and sharp desire. St. Nilus, who esteemed this metaphor, points out that like the rose bred among thorns, the Christian virtues are born among the beguilements of life.[36] It is a short distance between this analogy and the comparison of the rose to the Virgin Mary, the rose of roses, the miraculous flower of the thorn. Adam of St. Victor intones the hymn.

> Flos de spinis spina carens,
> Flos spineta gloria,
> Nos spinetum, nos peccati
> Spina sumus cruentati
> Sed tu spina nescia.[37]

[32] *Golden Legend*, trans. Caxton (London, 1900), VII, 45.
[33] XXXVII.970.
[34] Aldhelm, *Opera*, ed. Ehwald (Berlin, 1919), p. 430.
[35] Scottus, *Opera*, ed. Traube, *PLAC* (Berlin, 1896), III, 230–31.
[36] *Capita Paraenetica* (PG, LXXIX, 1257).
[37] *Opera* (PL, CXCVI, 1502). The authority behind the figure of the thorny Eve and the central theme of these lines rest on the tradition. I cite

It stands to reason that the son of the Virgin, the flower of
the tree of Jesse, is also the flower of the rose. The closed garden, says Dante, on which the light of Christ shone, brought
forth the rose in which the Divine Word is made flesh. "Quivi
è la rosa in che il Verbo Divino/ Carne si fece."[38] It is the
crown of thorns, agent of Christ's suffering and wounds, that
made firm the comparison between the greatest of the martyrs
and the flower, for Christ was one who grew among the thorns
of the world and knew their sharpness. To explain the relationship between blossom and God, Christian poets remade the
old legend of how white roses became red. Bion had written
that Venus, distracted by the death of Adonis, ran with her
bare feet through the white roses and stained them with her
blood.[39] Many centuries later, Walafridus Strabus wrote a
poem about the "merito florum flos" and said that the white
roses became red through the death of Christ, "Morte rosas
tinguens."[40] From the tenth century onward, Christ is frequently described as the mystic rose. "Bloom on our vine,
blessed Jesus, rose red and burning, red with the blood of passion, burning with the fire of love."[41] Thus the rose of fleeting
worldly pleasure is also the Christian and his God, a God who
is love, but who is also judge and sentencer. So there are two

two texts: "Eva ergo spina fuit, Maria rosa exstitit: Eva spina, vulnerando;
Maria rosa, omnium affectus mulcendo. Eva spina, infigens omnibus mortem:
Maria rosa redens salutiferam omnibus sortem" (Pseudo-Bernard, *De Beata
Maria Virgine Sermo* [PL, CLXXXIV, 1020]); and "Et velut e spinis
mollis rosa surgit acutis/ Nil quod laedat habens materemque obscurat
honore:/ Sic Evae de stirpe sacra veniente Maria/ Virginis antiquae facinus
nova Virgo piaret" (Sedulius, *Carmina*, ed. Huemer [Vienna, 1885], p. 46).
   [38] *Paradiso* XXIII.70–75.
   [39] I.19–22.
   [40] *Carmina*, ed. Duemmler, PLAC (Berlin, 1884), II. 348–49.
   [41] Pseudo- Bernard, *Vitis Mystica* (PL, CLXXXIV, 184, 708, 711, 715).
The theme of Christ the rose is prominent in Neo-Latin verse; see Joannes
Maior, "Rosa Imago Christi" and Frenzelius "Rosa Imago Christi," in
C. Dornavius, *Ampitheatrum* (Hanover, 1619), I, 193–94.

flowers, an earthly one and a heavenly one; and on this doctrine of the rose, the poem of Herbert rests.

The first part of the poem is obviously about two roses: the
Christian rose and the pagan rose, Christian and Mr. Worldly.
The latter rose, the symbol of feasting, drunkenness, passionate
love, and the joys and honors of the world has, before the
poem begins, been singing a rose song to the Christian rose
that lives among the thorns. This rose has "pass'd" its "rights
away" to what the worldly rose represents because it has returned to the Garden and risen from there to adorn the floor
of Heaven. But Herbert, the Christian rose, does not care for
a furious discussion of the two states of rosehood. He will be
quiet in this counterargument and show his opponent another
rose filled with the light of Christ. The literal rose that he re-
moves from his bosom and displays is at once Christian and
Christ. This is the life of the rose. It is, indeed, a rose that contains purgation—even the ancients knew that—but it is also
in its symbolic likeness a judge and a sentencer. For Herbert,
who in imitation of the Rose has renounced the roses of the
world, all pagan meanings of the rose, though known to him,
are valueless. He will not need the purge; he knows what the
sentence will be. The sickness of the rose can never infect
him now, for he can rely on the words of St. Peter as reported
in Acts 3:16—"And his name, through faith in his name, hath
made this man strong, whom ye see and know: yea, the faith
which is in him hath given this perfect health in the presence
of you all."

CHAPTER FIVE

Richard Lovelace

"The Grasse-Hopper"

This poem was written and sent by Lovelace to his fellow poet and royalist, Charles Cotton, sometime after the collapse of the great cause and the execution of King Charles. It is not unlikely that it was written by Lovelace in a moment of dejection after his own imprisonment and impoverishment. The story of the summer grasshopper that makes no provision for winter, that plays its violin while the ants are busy at harvest, obviously supplies the pre-text of the poem. The cavaliers were grasshoppers, and when this poem was written they were learning the lesson of the insect. Any reader can find all of this in "The Grasse-Hopper," and it is not surprising that the poem has been usually described as a simple cavalier lyric, a powerful overflow of alcoholic feelings recollected in adversity. But the poem is richer than it seems on first reading, and an examination of the tradition, of the metaphoric his-

tory of the insect that is the subject, will suggest that the
theme has emotional possibilities that have not been understood.

> Oh thou that swing'st upon the waving haire
>   Of some well-filled Oaten Beard,
> Drunke ev'ry night with a Delicious teare
>   Dropt thee from Heav'n, where now th'art reard.
>
> The Joyes of Earth and Ayre are thine intire,
>   That with thy feet and wings dost hop and flye;
> And when thy Poppy workes thou dost retire
>   To thy Carv'd Acron-bed to lye.
>
> Up with the Day, the Sun thou welcomst then,
>   Sportst in the guilt-plats of his Beames,
> And all these merry dayes mak'st merry men,
>   Thy selfe, and Melancholy streames.
>
> But ah the Sickle! Golden Eares are Cropt;
>   *Ceres* and *Bacchus* bid good night;
> Sharpe frosty fingers all your Flowr's have topt,
>   And what sithes spar'd, Winds shave off quite.
>
> Poore verdant foole! and now green Ice! thy Joys
>   Large and as lasting, as thy Peirch of Grasse,
> Bid us lay in 'gainst Winter, Raine, and poize
>   Their flouds, with an o'reflowing glasse.
>
> Thou best of *Men* and *Friends!* we will create
>   A Genuine Summer in each others breast;
> And spite of this cold Time and frosen Fate
>   Thaw us a warme seate to our rest.
>
> Our sacred harthes shall burne eternally
>   As Vestall Flames, the North-Wind, he
> Shall strike his frost-stretch'd Winges, dissolve and flye
>   This *Aetna* in Epitome.
>
> Dropping *December* shall come weeping in,
>   Bewayle th' usurping of his Raigne;

But when in show'rs of old Greeke we beginne,
Shall crie, he hath his Crowne againe!

Night as cleare *Hesper* shall our Tapers whip
From the light Casements where we play,
And the darke Hagge from her black mantle strip,
And sticke there everlasting Day.

Thus richer then untempted Kings are we,
That asking nothing, nothing need:
Though Lord of all what Seas imbrace; yet he
That wants himselfe, is poore indeed.

At first reading, the poem separates rather naturally into
two parts. Stanzas I–V set a familiar measure by recalling in a
submerged but personified fashion the literary ancestry of
the insect that is the subject. We recognize the subtune at
once; it is Anacreon, whose poem on the grasshopper had been
earlier translated by Belleau and Cowley. But Lovelace's poem
is no forthright rendering; it is a more complicated chorus of
voices. With the sixth stanza the imaginative rhythm begins
to alter, and not only is Horace heard, but there is also an
immediate contrast between the past and the present, between the symbolic history of the grasshopper and the immediate history of the poet and his friends. The prudent
morality of stanzas IV and V is rejected and, after a series of
variations, replaced by a Horatian act of will. In this artistic
voluntary there are both Christian and pagan tones. The
remedy for the moment is provided by the doctrine of Horace, although the inner conviction of an infinite present, once
satisfaction is procured, is totally Christian. This rough sum-
mation, however, must be annotated in terms of Lovelace's
gift from his predecessors.

Almost at the beginning of the history of poetic transformations, Anacreon of Teos heard the grasshopper in the fields of
summer and put him into song. He took delight in the insect

because it could be as drunk as a happy king on dew, because it owned all that it saw about it and took tribute from
the seasons. It is beloved of the Muses for its singing, he tells
us, and blessed by Phoebus; and if this is not merit enough,
the unsuffering song-lover is as ethereal as a god.

> Ἀπαθής δ', ἀναιμόσαρκος
> Σχεδὸν εἶ θεοῖς ὅμοιος.[1]

This in substance is what Anacreon wrote, and the first twelve
lines of Lovelace's poem [2] reproduce these themes against
a now universal landscape. But in these stanzas there is obviously more than a pleasant rewarming of Anacreon's poem,
and we do well to turn the hands of the poetic clock back-
ward for a better understanding.

Hesiod had also known the "blue-winged" grasshopper that
perched on green boughs, singing in the heat of the dog days
when the beard grew on the oats;[3] the grasshopper that made
sonorous odes in the luxuriant months when goats were fattest,
wine best, women amorous, and men languid.[4] It is, however,
Homer who creates a symbolic prejudice, when he compares
the song of the grasshopper to the "lily-like voices" of the
old Trojan aristocrats, who chattered on the wall as Queen
Helen walked through the wide-way to the Skaian Gate.[5]
From poems of this nature, the champions of Charles might
imagine that the grasshopper, the βασιλεύς of Anacreon, had

---

[1] XXXIV.17–18. The Greeks do not distinguish clearly between the
various singing insects, and it is not always clear what they mean when
they use τεττιξ, καλαμαια, μάντις, and ἀκρίς. The translators have done little
better, for Anacreon's poem is probably about the cicada.

[2] I have used the text of C. H. Wilkinson (Oxford, 1930). The two last
lines of the third stanza may be paraphrased as "days make men merry,
yourself merry, and melancholy streams away" or "make melancholy
streams (rivers) also merry."

[3] "Shield of Achilles," *Opera*, ed. Flach (Leipzig, 1878), pp. 393–400.

[4] *Theogony* 581–86.

[5] *Iliad* III.151–53.

aristocratic pretensions; if they did not heed the whisper of these texts, there were those that flatly stated the case. "It is only recently," Thucydides writes of the Athenians, "that their rich old men left off . . . fastening their hair with a tie of golden grasshoppers." [6] The so-called Suidas states that the grasshopper was the insignia of the Athenian nobles because not only was the insect a musician, but like Erechtheus, founder of the city, it was also born of the earth.[7] So the insect that sings throughout the rich and prosperous seasons of the year, the insect of warmth and light, is given the colors of wisdom possessed among the Greeks by the noblemen of Athens.

If for the Greeks the grasshopper is a symbol of the gay months and their magic, if he is also the representative in nature of the ἄριστοι, he is most triumphantly the analogue of the poet-singer, whose verses he so delicately graced throughout antiquity.[8] For this reason Meleager is securely in the tradition when he invokes the grasshopper as the "Muse of the cornlands" (ἀρουραίη Μοῦσα), the song writer of the dryads, the challenger in voice and verse of the great Pan.[9] In one ancient myth, a singing grasshopper, by alighting on the peg from which the lyre string had broken, helped Eunomos of Locris win the prize at the Pythian games by supplying the wanting notes.[10] Another legend, probably invented by Plato, may be used to fortify this one.

Once, when Socrates and Phaedrus were talking, the old philosopher heard the grasshoppers singing and said that they

[6] *History* I.6.

[7] *Historica* (Basel, 1564), col. 959.

[8] It is everywhere part of rural decoration; see Theocritus XVI.94–96; Vergil *Eclogues* II.12–13; *Georgics* III.328; "Culex" 151; *Copa* 27–28. The *Greek Anthology* is filled with poems to the grasshopper; see VII.189–94, 197–98, 201; IX.92.

[9] *Greek Anthology*, VII, 195–96.

[10] Strabo *Geography* VI.1, 9. Paulus Silentiarius (*G.A.*, VI, 54) puts this myth into elegant verse.

had received gifts from the gods which, in turn, they imparted to men. When the exquisite Phaedrus inquired about the nature of these gifts, Socrates related the following story:

A lover of the Muses should surely not be ignorant of this. It is said that once these grasshoppers were a race of men that lived before the Muses existed. When the Muses were born and song appeared, they were so moved by pleasure that as they sang, they forgot to eat and death caught them unawares. They live now in the grasshoppers, having that boon from their birth until their death. When they die, they inform the Muses in Heaven who worships them here below. Terpsichore, they tell of those who have honored her in the dance, and thus make them dearer to her; Erato, they tell of her lovers and to each sister they report according to her honorers. But to Calliope, the eldest, and to Urania, the second of the nine, they bear tidings of those who pass their lives in philosophic study and the observance of their special music; for these are the Muses, who having Heaven for their particular sphere and words both human and divine, speak most gladly.[11]

So with Plato, whose own musical voice was likened by Timon [12] to the "lily-songs" of the Hecademian grasshoppers, the insects become the apotheoses of human singers who have lost their lives through their love of art. "Dropt thee from Heav'n, where now th'art reard." The insect—Plato's myth and Anacreon's poem intermarry—is now a poet, and the evidence of its transformation, with a further qualification, is found in the writings of Flavius Philostratus.

Among the letters of the author of *Apollonius* and the *Imagines,* books popular with men of the Renaissance, is one commending the poet Celsus to a wealthy patron. This poet, Philostratus writes, has, "as do the good grasshoppers [οἱ

[11] *Phaedrus* 259. I cannot find this legend in any text prior to Plato's; Photius mentions it as if it were common knowledge (*Bibliotheca* [PG, CIII, 1354]).

[12] Diogenes Laertius *Lives* III.7.

χρηστοὶ τέττιγες], devoted his life to song; you will see to it that he is fed on more substantial food than dew." [13] At the touch of metaphor the poet is made a grasshopper; but in the *Apollonius*, Philostratus associates the grasshopper with the plight of men who have lost out. The philosopher Demetrius, exiled to Dicaearchia by the Roman despot, cries out in envy of the singing insects and says to Apollonius that they, at least, are never in danger of persecution and are above human calumny, for they have been set aloft by the Muses so that they "might be the blissful poets of that felicity which is theirs." [14] This comparison of Demetrius is close to the central tone of "The Grasse-Hopper."

By following the tradition through antiquity, we come on imaginative identifications that help us read this seventeenth-century poem. We know that the grasshopper was beloved of the Muses; that it had once been a human artist and continued to accompany and instruct human artists; that it was a king, an aristocrat, a badge of royalty, a poet; and that it was iden-tified with men in political disfavor. This multiple suggestive-ness may explain why Cowley translated Anacreon's poem and why Lovelace sought to remake it into something at once familiar yet novel. When we read the first three stanzas of Lovelace's poem, all that we have learned from the Greeks is born again. The grasshopper is drunk on dew, now a "Deli-cious teare"; he swings from the oaten beard on which Hesiod had placed him; but like the song-obsessed Platonic grass-hoppers, he has been "reard" to Heaven. We see at once be-hind the literal front, for we know that the grasshopper is an aristocrat, a King. We have been reading a poem about a King and a cause that are dead on earth but living in Heaven. The poem has nothing to do with grasshoppers.

Choosing what in many respects was an optimistic symbol,

[13] *Opera*, ed. Kayser (Leipzig, 1870), p. 364.
[14] *Ibid.*, p. 261.

Lovelace annotated it with melancholia. According to the bright Attic tradition, as represented by the poem of Meleager, the grasshopper's music was the anodyne of sorrow, and Lovelace remembers this in the latter lines of the third stanza. But the living grasshopper of the Greek solar months is made a poetic prelude to the inexperienced innocent, "poore verdant foole," who is in Heaven. In this interplay of life and death, tersely suggested by stanzas IV and V, we pass from what is light and warm into the cold darkness of inescapable defeat and death.

> But ah the Sickle! Golden Eares are Cropt;
> *Ceres* and *Bacchus* bid good night;
> Sharpe frosty fingers all your Flowr's have topt,
> And what sithes spar'd, Winds shave off quite.
>
> Poore verdant foole! and now green Ice! thy Joys
> Large and as lasting, as thy Peirch of Grasse,
> Bid us lay in 'gainst Winter, Raine, and poize
> Their flouds, with an o'reflowing glasse.

The quiet warning of the first stanza, which had been further muted by the bright Anacreontic quatrains, is now made into a torrent of trumpets. Behind the allegory of nature and the classical figments, the emotional current of the decade in which the poem was written comes plain. The grasshopper King, who symbolically loved the sun, has been harvested with the harvest. The flowers of his realm are topped by the "sithes" or, spared by these, shaved by the cruel winds. The merry men, faced by winter, look to the lesson of the summer singer. At this point, too, the poet makes his own self-identifications, for all that antiquity had attributed to the grasshopper—the sign of the aristocrat, the symbol of the poet singer, and the man in political ill favor—suit him. The emphasis is solemn enough and with it Lovelace remembers many things. He recalls, perhaps, the legend of the impotent Ti-

thonus, but he expresses the tragedy of the summer-happy insect with that prudent variant of the Aesopica.[15] He leaves
the myrtles and laurels of the Greek sea islands to inhabit for
a while the north of cold and sunlessness.

In the gathering shadows of the world of death we hear for
a moment an ancient funeral chant. The crops are harvested.
Ceres and Bacchus have departed to a deeper sleep than that
enjoyed by the sunlight grasshopper when its "Poppy
workes." Winter has frozen even Fate. The North Wind
strikes with "his frost-stretch'd Winges." December comes in
tears far different from those that "Dropt thee from Heav'n."
Sullenly, the "darke Hagge" hangs about "light Casements."
Anacreon's season is over. Nature is now sternly present,
thinly veiling with her realities the parallel actualities of the
poet's life. We leave the dark external world to enter the
poet's heart. In this black moment of cold, the Christian tone
begins, for Lovelace remembers the once bright celebration
of the wintered year.

> Dropping *December* shall come weeping in,
>   Bewayle th' usurping of his Raigne;
> But when in show'rs of old Greeke we beginne,
>   Shall crie, he hath his Crowne againe!

Pathos and hope, together with December memories of the
Roman Saturnalia, are joined in this somberly happy stanza,
but to increase its emotion we must remember the Christmas
prince, who wore his crown during the festivities of the Christ-

[15] The fable of the industrious ant and the careless grasshopper was
popularized in the Middle Ages by Alexander Neckham (*Novus Aesopus*
XXIX). It also appears in various French redactions; see J. Bastin, *Recueil
General des Isopets* (Paris, 1929), and Marie de France, *Poesies*, ed. De
Roquefort (Paris, 1832), II, 123–25. Seneca suggests the legend in *Epistolae
Morales* LXXXVII.19–20. The early Fathers think of the insect in the
metaphoric manner of the poets (Ambrose, *Hexameron* [PL, XIV, 251–52]),
or commend it for some Christian quality (Gregory, *Oratio* [PG, XXXVI,
59]; and Jerome, *Epistulae* XXII.18).

mas week as proudly as Charles had worn his.[16] But the royalty of Christmas, shared by all who kept the feast, had been despoiled, as the royalists were despoiled, by the new masters of the state. For a number of years John Evelyn recorded the dismal fall of the Christmas king. One of his entries reads: "Christmasday, no sermon any where, no church being permitted to be open, so observed it at home." [17]

Lovelace's solution, like Evelyn's, is based on privacy and withdrawal. The aristocratic poets may be the victims of a frosty fortune, but they can "create/ A Genuine Summer in each others breast," a summer that inwardly is more real than the winters of Nature and Fate. So when December comes lamenting the usurping of "his Raigne," the "his" means both the King of England and the King of Christmas. To emend this tragic state, Lovelace and Cotton can make bowers in each other's breasts where the two rejected kings may dwell with them. By this act of the imagination, Christian in its import (for "the Kingdom of Heaven is within you"), they will privately establish a reality greater than the facts allow. To the winter rains, which are December's tears as opposed to those that banished Ceres wept for the crops, the poets will offer a counterblast, "show'rs of old Greeke," wine and, perhaps, the Greek point of view. Both they and the mourning month can then say of the two dead kings, "he hath his Crowne againe."

It could be said that "The Grasse-Hopper," in spite of these more subtle undertones, is simply a cavalier drinking song,

[16] The career of such a prince, who had in his titles the distinction of "high Regent of the Hall" (probably Gloucester Hall, Lovelace's college) has come down to us in an eyewitness account; see G. Higgs, *An Account of the Christmas Prince, as it was exhibited in the University of Oxford in the year 1607* (London, 1816).

[17] See the *Diary* (De Beer edition) for December 25 in 1652, 1654, 1655. The parliamentary order of December 19, 1644, abolished the observance of Christmas.

not unlike Cotton's "Chanson à Boire" or "Clepsydra." Alco-
hol had always been a cavalier cure, and Alexander Brome
can advise his friends to seek refuge in wine, "in big-bellied
bowls," "true philosophy lies in the bottle." Some of this
drunken logic certainly seeps into Lovelace's poem; in fact,
it is the ostensible mode. We must not forget that the poem,
though it began in death, passed into warmth and light, that
though we are now in the night and the cold, we shall emerge
into an eternal beatitude that will cancel temporal despair.
A consciousness of eternity is present in this poem even when
the metaphors of death and despair are paraded in stanzas IV
and V; it comes resolutely forward in "Our sacred harthes
shall burne eternally/ As Vestall Flames." Opposed to the
North Wind, the savage symbol of death and evil, are the
virginal fires of the ever burning hearth within the human
heart. This is the kingdom of the heart—this "Aetna in Epit-
ome"; but it is also something that cannot be lost because it
is something "we will create." The general state has perished
and Lovelace proposes to replace it with another state, one
that is inner, private.

The kingdom of the heart that Lovelace would restore is
not one of retreat and withdrawal, the resolution in isolation
that charmed so many of his fellow sufferers; [18] it is rather
a revision of his own cosmogony. The hovering emblem of
the winged North Wind, against which Lovelace directs the
symbolic fires of the "sacred harthes," makes firm this revision; for Lovelace must have seen in Aquilo, as Milton did,
the bony face of death. The wind that the ancients called "hor-
risonus," "saevus," "ferus," "horrifer," and "crudelis" was a
bitter symbol for this generation. Evil was North, from

[18] On the cavaliers' praise of solitude as an escape from the evils of the
Commonwealth, see H. G. Wright, "The Theme of Solitude and Retirement in Seventeenth Century Literature," Études Anglaises, VII (1954),
22–35.

whence streamed the gonfalon of death, a banner that men said blew significantly "ab sinistro." [19] The vestal fires that blast with their heart heat the North and the cold, the "show'rs of old Greeke" that dry up tears and rain, are augmented in their symbolic services by the display of lights that whip the "darke Hagge" of Night from "the light Casements." Within themselves, the frozen poets will remake the lost summer of the grasshopper. It is more than a lost summer; it is a shore of light as Vaughan would have understood it. This will be done, Lovelace informs Cotton, by means of candles as potent as the planet Venus, the "cleare *Hesper*." They are candles in the way that the fire is a fire; in one sense they are wax, in another, they are an inward light. By them Night is stripped forever of her dark cloak, for they will "sticke there everlasting Day." The warmth and brightness of the grasshopper's year, realized literally and, consequently, finitely in the early part of the poem are thus made eternal. The poet puts down Gothic horror; the grasshopper is made immortal; antique fearlessness is restored.

With the last stanza, the king, who has until now been hidden from us by a series of artistic translucencies, is revealed in his clear title. He is more than king of the summer fields or of Britain, for in governing the world of his creative imagination, he is untempted by the world. The poet and his friend, who may also be the "himselfe" of the last line, have created a kingdom privately. This kingdom cannot go down because it is invincible to outward attack. With this last stanza, the Horatian music that we have heard steadily since the dreary center of stanza V seems to achieve symphonic fullness. We have the impression of the Horatian tone because we know it has to be here. Horace, who fought on the wrong side

[19] For some associations, see St. Augustine, *In Iobam*, ed. Zycha (Vienna, 1895), p. 608 and his *Epistulae*, ed. Goldbacher (Vienna, 1904), p. 201; see also Eucherius, *Liber Formularum* (*PL*, L, 740–41).

at Philippi, must have appeared to Lovelace and Cotton as a
Roman cavalier who, when all was lost, found the good way.
His metaphors repeat themselves once more. The tempest
comes with the rain and the North Wind, but one forgets them
before a heaped fire and a full cup.

> Horrida tempesta caelum contraxit, et imbres
>   Nivesque deducunt Iovem; nunc mare, nunc silvae
> Threicio Aquilone sonant. Rapiamus, amici,
>   Occasionem de die, dumque virent genua
> Et decet, obducta solvatur fronte senectus.
>   Tu vina Torquato move consule pressa meo.
> Cetera mitte loqui: deus haec fortasse benigna
>   Reducet in sedem vice.[20]

In Horace's poetic promises there is little eternity; this illusion
is shunned. The fire on the Sabine hearth is as real as the wind
and the rain. It is Lovelace who creates the illusion for which
he lives. In another sense "himselfe" may not be Cotton at all,
but the private world of the poet's heart, where all is warm and
light and the grasshopper lives in a kingdom made eternal by
his song.

[20] *Epodes* XIII.1–8; *Carmina* I.9.5–8, 13–14; 17; 18; II.7, 11.

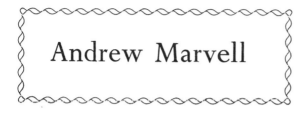

CHAPTER SIX

Andrew Marvell

"The Nymph Complaining
for the Death of Her Faun"

The poem that Marvell shows us is about a "nymph," and unless he uses this word with indecorous irony, she is a young virgin, who lives in a world of pastoral innocence different from the world of "cruel men." Into this "little Wilderness," which is not a wilderness at all, has come a man with the significant name of Sylvio (no wonder "he grew wild"), who has won the girl's love. The fawn, which Sylvio gives the girl as a token of love becomes, when he abandons her, a *surrogatus amoris;* in fact, it becomes something like the child that might have been hers had Sylvio not proved "counterfeit." The poem is not, as critics have said, about kindness to animals, or the death of Christ, or the British Church; on the contrary, it is a sensitive treatment of the loss of first love, a loss augmented by a virginal sense of deprivation and unfulfillment.

The nymph has brooded so much over losing her lover that she
has enlarged the token of love into a life symbol.
The mode of the poem is as honest as its literal reading. It
is a pastoral epicedium recited while the creature that it celebrates dies. This is a new notion—to preach the funeral sermon before the heart stops and the breath is gone. To assure
us about the nature of the poem, Marvell calls it a "complaint,"
putting it in a recognized poetic tradition. The topics that
govern the formal complaint are altered because its subject is
an animal. Even then, the physical and moral qualities of. the
fawn are mentioned; its death is described, and its immortality
is promised. The fawn has "virgin Limbs"; it is white and loving; it is light-footed and fleet. It lies among lilies and devours
roses. It is promised a tomb and an eternity, "in fair Elizium to
endure." All of these expressions are adaptations of the normal
themes previously applied to men, and they had been used before when the death of a beloved creature was lamented.
    Complaints on the deaths of favorite animals fill the seventh
book of the Greek Anthology,[1] but Marvell's readers would
be more likely to remember Catullus' lament on the death of
Lesbia's sparrow, a bird similar in some of its ways to the fawn
but different in its fate.

> Nam mellitus erat suamque norat
> Ipsam tam bene quam puella matrem;
> Nec sese a gremio illius movebat,
> Sed circumsiliens modo huc modo illuc
> Ad solam dominam usque pipiabat.[2]

---

[1] VII, 189–92, 194–203, 207–16; see the Supplement, ed. Dübner (Paris,
1890), II, 387. For imitations of Catullus' poem in English, see J. A. S.
McPeek, Catullus in Strange and Distant Britain (Cambridge, Mass., 1939),
pp. 61–72; the author of this monograph was the first to notice the connection between Marvell and Catullus.
[2] III.6–10.

The fawn, too, would "stay, and run again, and stay"; it, too, nursed at the nymph's finger and kissed her mouth. The echoes of Catullus' poem combine also with Ovid's lament over Corinna's popinjay, a bird famous for his color and voice, and in its way a symbol of mortal existence. "Plena fuit vobis omni concordia vita,/ Et stetit ad finem longa tenaxque fides." For the tomb of this pet, so closely associated with the love and life of his mistress, Ovid wrote an epitaphic couplet in which he assured his readers that it was not excluded from Elizium, "whither Swans and Turtles go."

> Colle sub Elysio nigra nemus ilice frondens,
>   Udaque perpetuo gramine terra, viret.
> Si qua fides dubiis; volucrum locus ille piarum
>   Dicitur, obscoenae quo prohibentur aves.
> Illic innocui late pascuntur olores;
>   Et vivax phoenix, unica semper avis.
> Explicat ipsa suas ales Junonia pennas:
>   Oscula dat cupido blanda columba mari.
> Psittacus has inter, nemorali sede receptus,
>   Convertit volucres in sua verba pias.[3]

A classically trained reader might remember these obvious texts and incorporate them as silent stanzas in this poem; but he might also ask himself why, with all of this tradition behind him, Marvell selected a fawn instead of a more ordinary creature for the immediate center of the nymph's complaint.

The literary antecedents once again supply us with a reading of Marvell's literal statement. The first of them, as Muir[4] pointed out, is from the seventh book of the *Aeneid*,[5] where the death of Silvia's pet deer at the hands of Ascanius is re-

[3] *Amores* II.6; for other earlier texts, see Herrlinger, *Totenklage um Tiere in der Antiken Dichtung* (Stuttgart, 1930).
[4] *Notes and Queries*, CXCVI (1951), 115.
[5] VII.475–504.

lated. It is also a tamed wild thing that has wandered into the
human world and been wantonly slain. The penalty for this
rash killing was the war between the Teucrians and the men
of Latium. In the second book [6] of the epic, there are some
oblique lines that remind us of Agamemnon's destruction of
Artemis' deer, a thoughtless act that brought death to Iphigenia in the depressing version of her myth. Sophocles'
Electra also informs us that the giant king, "once disporting
himself in the grove of the goddess," startled the dappled animal and boastingly shot it. For this impiety, he paid with his
daughter's blood.[7] In neither case is the deer made the subject
of a formal lamentation; nevertheless, the menace is made clear
and the nymph's "They cannot thrive" is illuminated by these
poetic predecessors.

In both of the older legends, the slaughtered deer is more
a thing of the woods than the nymph's fawn, "Ty'd in this
silver chain and Bell"; hence, it is pleasant to come on the
ancestor of Marvell's fawn in the eclogues of Calpurnius,
where the pastor Astilius, who wagers the animal in a singing
contest, calls attention to its excellence.

> en aspicis illum,
> Candida qui medius cubat inter lilia cervum?
> Quamvis hunc Petale mea diligat, accipe victor.
> Scit frenos et ferre iugum, sequiturque vocantem
> Credulus, et mensae non improba porrigit ora.
> Aspicis, ut fruticat late caput, utque sub ipsis
> Cornibus et tereti pendent redimicula collo?
> Aspicis, ut niveo frons irretita capistro
> Lucet, et a dorso, quae totam circuit alvum,
> Alternat vitreas lateralis cingula bullas?

[6] II.116–17.
[7] VII.565–72; see Hyginus 98; Arnobius V.34; Servius, *ad loc*. Dictys says
that the animal was a "capra," (*De Historia Belli Troiana* [Venice, 1499],
B2v); Antonius Liberalis, 27, states that Artemis supplied a deer in the
place of Iphigenia.

Cornua subtiles ramosque tempora molles
Implicuere rosae, rutiloque monilia torque
Extrema cervice natant, ubi pendulus apri
Dens sedet, et nivea distinguit pectora luna.[8]

Marvell's nymph would know this deer—a lounger among lilies; his horns are wrapped in roses; and he has his collar and ornaments. He is, however, a wanderer, for he has strayed from the deer park of the *Metamorphoses*.

Marvell must have remembered the deer beloved by Cyparissus, the handsome friend of Apollo. The Ovidian deer has golden horns ("cornua fulgebant auro"), and a collar of gems and a silver bell. "Bulla super frontem parvis argentea loris/ Vincta movebatur." Its ears are hung with pearls, and it is exceedingly tame. It frequents houses ("celebrare domos"), allows strangers to stroke it, and is the possessive joy of its master, who leads it to brooks in fair pastures, adorns it with flowers ("texebas varios per cornua flores"), and rides on its back. This deer is inadvertently killed, not by wanton hunters, but by Cyparissus, who is so overwhelmed by grief that he resolves to die. His patron-god, in pity, changes him, not into a memorial statue, but into the tree that is the symbol of grief.

Ingemuit, tristisque Deus, "Lugebere nobis,
Lugebisque alios, aderisque dolentibus," inquit.[9]

[8] VI.32–45.

[9] X.106–42. The association between the Artemis of the Agamemnon legend and the Apollo of the Ovidian account is made in the myth of Hercules' fifth labor, the capture of the deer of Ceryneia. This animal, with horns of gold and hoofs of bronze, was formerly dedicated to Artemis by the nymph Tagete, and Hercules, having captured it, was halted by the goddess and her brother and forced into an excuse (Apollodorus II.5.3; Euripides *Her. Fur.* ll. 378 ff.). The deer had earlier escaped from Artemis, when she captured its four fellows for her team (Callimachus III.97–109), and, according to Pindar (*Olymp.* III.50–52) wore a collar on which the nymph had inscribed the goddess' name. In the pseudo-Aristotelian περι Θαυμασιον Ακουσματον (110), we are informed that Agathocles of Sicily

Marvell's fawn is, perhaps, the offspring of these poetic recollections which seem to dominate and pervade the whole
poem, and we, as informed readers, will probably use some
of them. The first twenty-four lines of the poem make a
hymn, an opening liturgical phrase, and here the fawn has
special meaning; for we are led, as the song mounts in our
minds, into a numinous world where the wild things of the
wood are associated with the wild things of the solitary human
heart. The archaic word "deodand" establishes a ritualistic
emphasis for these lines, even though the betrayed nymph
reverses the usual definition of the word. The act of killing is
an act of impiety. Fawns are never slain; deer are killed in
season with ritual; and the butchery of the dead animal, in the
course of which the hands of the hunt master are washed in
blood, is a matter of extreme ceremony.[10] The "wanton
troopers" are unworthy of the hunt, which is made plain by
their ignorance of ceremony; hence they are both "ungentle
men" and "ungentlemen." Through their foul act, a quasi-
religious ritual has been debased and reduced to horrid slaughter. "Beasts must be with justice slain"; so a penalty must be

---

captured a deer wearing a collar marked with the name of Artemis. There
are other legends of deer with collars. Solinus (XIX.18) reports the capture
of a deer wearing the collar of Alexander, and collared deer appear in
the sonnets of Romanello and Petrarch. Mezeray, *Histoire de France*
(Paris, 1643), I, 930, contains an account of a deer captured in 1381 by
Charles VI with a collar on which was written "Hoc me Caesar donavit."
The allegorical deer of Fida in Brown's *Eclogues* mentioned by Bradbrook
and Lloyd Thomas in *Andrew Marvell* (Cambridge, 1940), and accepted by
Margoliouth in his notes to the *Poems* (1952) has, I think, very little to
do with this poem. One would do better to recall the Capuan deer of
Silius Italicus (XIII. 115-37), "quae candore nivem, candore anteiret olores."
It came readily to be stroked, combed, and bathed; it was thought to be
a familiar of Diana and the divine spirit of the city. It was killed by the
Roman general without serious consequences.

[10] *Le Livre de Chasse du Roy Modus*, ed. Tilander (Paris, 1931), pp. 7-43;
G. Turbervil, *The Noble Arte of Venerie or Hunting* (Oxford, 1907)
pp. 39-143.

paid and the nymph knows this well. The Capuan deer of Silius Italicus was killed for a just sacrifice, and Artemis could substitute a deer to save the person of Iphigenia, but the death of the nymph's fawn cannot "do them any good." It repeats the woodland crimes of Ascanius and Agamemnon.

The subject of the hymn has further meaning, because deer are blessed creatures. In classical texts they are sometimes revealed as spirits in animal form. Livy tells a legend of divine deer,[11] and Pausanius repeats two stories in which deer are workers of miracles.[12] During the Middle Ages, the sacred nature of deer was recorded in literary texts. It was a sacred deer, according to Benôit de Sainte-More,[13] who brought Paris to be judge in the contest between the three goddesses. Raimbert de Paris tells us that a deer, "blans come nois," showed Charlemagne the St. Bernard Pass, and that the great king considered the animal as God's messenger. "Ves le message que Dex a envoie." [14] In *Les Saisnes*, a fellow of this deer leads the great King to the only passage in the dangerous Rune.

> Qant ce voit l'empereres, n' i ot point de deshait;
> "Or quide il qe Dex por mostrance, l'ait fait,
> La ou cers ala, soit merchie et portrait." [15]

The more ordinary champions of the mediaeval romances were also associated in supernatural fashion with the holy deer. In the *Geste de Nanteuil*, the child Tristan is rescued from cruel fisherfolk by a deer that carried him into the forest and there looked to his nurture.[16] The knight Tyolet, who was brought up by his fearful mother in ignorant seclusion, learns

---

[11] X.27.8–10.
[12] II.30.7 and VIII.22.9.
[13] *Roman de Troie*, ed. Constans (Paris, 1904), ll. 3860–68.
[14] *Le Chevalerie Ogier de Danemarche*, ed. Barrois (Paris, 1842), pp. 11–12.
[15] Eds. Menzel and Stengel (Marburg, 1906), pp. 190–91. Similar legends are told about Clovis (Mezeray I.35).
[16] Paul Meyer, "Notice sur le roman de Tristan de Nanteuil," *Jahresbuch für Rom. u. Engl. Literatur*, IX (1868), 4–42.

about chivalry from a magic deer that "se transfigura. . . . / Et unchevalier resembloit." [17] But the most noteworthy experience with strange deer is that of Guigemar, who wounded a white doe and was retributively wounded himself when the arrow rebounded. The dying animal begins to speak French and tells the hunter that he will not be cured of his wound until he suffers much for a woman who has endured more than any other of her sex.[18] The mysteriousness of white deer is further enhanced by an episode in *Godefroid de Bouillon*, which narrates the rescue of Harpin by his friend Carbaran, who was led to the place of danger by three deer—not deer exactly, but "Seignor, c'estoit Saint Joires, Saint Barles, Saint Domis." [19] Some of these poetical precedents help us to understand the lines: "O help O help: I see it faint:/ And dye as calmely as a Saint." We also begin to realize why the nymph proposes placing a golden vial of the deer's tears as a reliquary in the shrine of Diana, patron saint of deer.

The association of deer with holy men does much to explain the under-chorus of the first hymn sung by the nymph, an under-chorus so vibrant that some critics have mistaken it for the whole poem. Probably the oldest legend that brings deer and sainthood together is that of St. Eustace or St. Placidas. It is found in prose in the *Acta Graeca* [20] and other calendars, but it was given poetic reality by an unknown poet of the Carolingian age.

> Dum esset magnus venator et saggittarius,
> Die quadam exivit more venancium;
> Aspexit grandem a longe cervorum numerum

---

[17] G. Paris, "Lais Inédits," *Romania*, VIII (1879), 43. In similar fashion, Richard of Normandy, hastening to deliver a message to Charlemagne, is shown the ford of the River Flagot by a white deer (*Fierabras*, eds. Kroeber and Servois [Paris, 1860], p. 132).

[18] Marie de France, *Lais*, ed. Warnke (Halle, 1925), pp. 9–10.

[19] *La Chanson du Chevalier au Cygne et de Godefroid de Bouillon*, ed. Hippeau (Paris, 1877), p. 264.

[20] *Analecta Bollandiana*, III (1884), 68–70.

Et unum candidum nimis stantem in medio:
Cepit persequi illum relictis omnibus.

Dum per spacia multa post eum curreret,
Ascendit cervus in summum saxorum verticem.
Placidas dum perpensaret, quid illi faceret,
Vidit in cornibus eius crucis imaginem
Et inter cornua pulcram Christi effigiem.

Placidas dum stupendo istud aspiceret,
Vocem sibi dicentem audivit taliter:
"Placidas, O Placidas, quid me persequeris?
Iesus ego, nescis quem fide credere,
Sed in operibus bonis visus es colere." [21]

The experience of Saint Placidas puts that of St. Giles or St. Godric,[22] who are more commonly associated with deer, in the shadow; and the conversion of this man, who became a martyr, is paralleled in literature by that of the father of the mediaeval French hero, Doon of Maience. In the *Romance of Doon*, we read that his father, hunting in the forest, slew with the same arrow a deer and its hermit master. In penitence for this deed, the hunter gave up chivalry and devoted his full service to God.[23] All of these accounts make it clear that salvation can come to a thoughtless hunter through the intermediation of the white deer, Jesus Christ.

The deer as the symbol of Christ was known to the Fathers and Doctors of the Church,[24] and the literary manifestations

---

[21] *Rythmi aevi Merovingici et Carolini*, ed. Winterfeld, PLAC (Berlin, 1899), IV, 593–94. See the English version in J. L. Weston, *Chief Middle English Poets* (Boston, 1914), pp. 78–79.

[22] For St. Giles and his deer, see *Analect. Boll.*, VIII (1889), 111–12, and the poetic "La Vie de Saint Giles" of Guillaume de Berneville, eds. Paris and Bos (Paris, 1881), pp. 46–52. For St. Godric, see Reginald of Coldingham, *Libellus de vita et miraculis S. Godrici* (London, 1847), p. 96.

[23] Ed. Pey (Paris, 1859), pp. 3–4.

[24] The deer is Christ: "imo cervi cervorum, id est Christi," writes Bede in *Psalmorum Librum Exegesis* (PL, XCIII, 702–703). There are many patristic references of this nature and the bestiaries also support it.

of the symbol were often brilliantly stated. According to one
pious legend, a deer similar to the one that reproached St.
Placidas appeared to two other saints in the forest of Brie, and
subsequently reappeared in the presence of the whole congre-
gation when these two holy men were assisting the Pope at
mass in the Lateran.[25] The most charming literary account of
the deer-Christ is that of Malory. Galahad, Percival, Bors, and
Percival's sister are in a forest and see a white hart led by four
lions entering a chapel, where a good hermit sings the mass of
the Holy Ghost.

> And at the secrets of the mass, they saw the hart become a
> man, the which marvelled them, and set him upon the altar in
> a rich siege, and saw the four lions were changed, the one to
> the form of a man, the other to the form of a lion, and the
> third to an eagle, and the fourth was changed unto an ox.
> Then took they their siege where the hart sat, and went out
> through a glass window, and there was nothing perished nor
> broken, and they heard a voice say, In such a manner entered
> the son of God into the womb of a maid Mary.

The astonished watchers seek the full meaning of the moving
symbols from a hermit, who informs them:

> And well ought our Lord be signified to an hart; for the
> hart when he is old he waxeth young again in his white skin:
> right so cometh again our Lord from death to life, for he lost
> earthly flesh, that was the deadly flesh which he had taken
> in the womb of the blessed virgin Mary; and for that cause
> appeared our Lord as a white hart without spot. . . . For wit
> ye well never erst might no knight know the truth, for, ofttimes
> ere this, our Lord shewed him unto good men and unto good
> knights in the likeness of an hart.[26]

[25] Pierre Hélyot, *Histoire des Ordres Monastiques* (Paris, 1714–1719),
II, 127–29.
[26] *Le Morte Darthur*, ed. Strachey (London, 1912), p. 399. For previous
interpretations of this poem, see the bibliography cited by E. S. LeComte,
"Marvell's 'The Nymph Complaining for the Death of Her Faun,'" *MP*,

The assurances of the "good man in a religious weed, and in the armour of our Lord" have already been supported by symbolic examples in the metrical romances.

There is no doubt that the opening hymn of the nymph's epicedium contains a clear allusion to the "hinnulus cervorum," the name that St. Gregory gave to Christ. The innocence of the white fawn, the wantonness and injustice of the death, the washing of the hands, the reference to "Heaven's King," the sense of sacrifice and atonement, the concluding, "There is not such another in/ This World to offer for their Sin," point dramatically at this symbolic equivalent. But we should be aware that this subsurface suggestion is metaphoric rather than symbolic. The poem is not to be read as a mediaeval text, but as one in the baroque manner. The nymph who cries that even her own blood, which flows from her broken heart, is also not enough, "Yet could they not be clean," is not given to sacrilege. The poem is not about Christ. The deer is *like* Christ; it is not Christ. The poetic process that Marvell is here employing can be illustrated in reverse by two passages from the *Christiados* of Vives, who uses the metaphor of the hunted deer to explain the suffering of tormented holy ones. In the first, we witness the accusal of Susanna:

> Stabat conspectu in medio tremebunda puella,
> Iam suffusa oculos mortis nigrore propinquae,
> Et positis terram genibus submissa petebat:
> Non minus exanimata metu, quam in retia cerva
> Acta canum latratu, et longo exercita cursu,
> Cum iam consumptae vires, cum se undique cinctam
> Hoste videt, mortemque instantem certa moratur.[27]

L (1952), 97–101 and K. Williamson, "A Reply," *MP*, LI (1954), 268–71. For more recent proposals, see E. H. Emerson's article and Pierre Legouis' response in *Études Anglaises*, VIII (1955), 107–12 and "Marvell's 'Nymph Complaining for the Death of Her Faun': Sources versus Meaning," by Leo Spitzer in *MLQ*, XIX (1958), 231–43.

[27] *Opera* (Venice, 1538), p. 28.

The second passage shows us Christ before the Jews:

> veluti aspexit si forte Magistri
> Assuetum imperiis cervum media urbe Molossus,
> Sylvestrem ratus insequitur, vix voce coercet
> Venator rabido instantem cervicibus ore.[28]

In both of these instances, the figure is part of the lyrical flow and shares only obliquely in the full meaning; the martyrs are "like deer" and not deer.

The use of the Christ or saint metaphor is restricted to the complaining nymph, who is one person removed from the poet; the poet, on the other hand, employs the fawn in another metaphoric situation which the reader must understand to grasp the complexity of the poem. The implied metaphor supports the earlier decision that the animal is a *surrogatus amoris* and establishes a second point in the belief that the verse itself alternates between the secular and the divine, the classical and the Christian, in its literary allusiveness.

The poets of antiquity, it is well known, associated the deer with metaphors of love. Oppian finds them as emblematic of passion as birds;[29] and Theocritus' lovesick Cyclops feeds eleven fawns for the beloved but disdainful Galathea.[30] Horace compares his evasive Chloe to a frightened fawn ("Vitas inuleo me similis, Chloe"); assures her that he will not crush her as a lion or tiger would; and urges her to leave her mother and submit to him.[31] We find the two parts of the classical simile brought together in the fifteenth century *Gloria d'Amor* of Fra Rocaberti, who associates lovers with the hunting of the deer.

[28] *Ibid.,* p. 61.
[29] *Cynegetica* II.186–205. The metaphor is also used by Callimachus (*Epig.* 33), and by Agathias (*G.A.* V.292) whose girl-fawn is surrounded by roses and doves.
[30] *Eclogae* XI.40–41.
[31] *Carmina* I.23.

Com per lo giny del exercit de cassa
Los servos braus passen per via certa,
E qui. ls vol mort per lo fill los acassa
Axi viu jo per una selv' escura
Gran gent venir, arreglats a parella,
Vencuts d'amor; conegui lur figura,
Ab cants e lays de piedosa planta
Mostrant amor esser lur amat temple.[32]

In French literature of the sixteenth and seventeenth centuries, the game of love as a deer hunt, the beloved as a deer,
and the lover as a wounded deer are common metaphoric
equations. Marot makes one of these comparisons in his epi-
grams: "Les cerfz en rut pour les les bisches se battent,/ Les
amoureux pour les dames combattent." [33] A little later, Ronsard frames his "Amours d'Eurymedon et Callirée" against
the background of a deer hunt. The early seventeenth century saw the appearance of an anonymous "La Chasse et
l'Amour"; [34] and Jean Passerat wrote a symbolic poem, "Le
Cerf d'Amour," [35] and followed the analogy in "Sur la Com-
paraison des Cerfs et de Amoureaux."

Le Cerf et l'amoureaux, d'une diverse flame
Qu'allume un mesme Dieu, sont egaux en malheur:
L'un souffre maint travail, l'autre mainte douleur:
L'un court apres sa biche, et l'autre apres sa Dame. . . .
O Cerfs a quatre pieds, nous sommes vos parens,
Nous les Cerfs a deux pies qu'Amour a rendu bestes.[36]

[32] Ed. Heaton (New York, 1916), pp. 75–76.
[33] *Œuvres*, ed. Janet (Paris, 1873), III, 54.
[34] *Variétés Historiques et Littéraires*, ed. Fournier (Paris, 1855), I, 65–73.
[35] *Les Poesies Françaises*, ed. Blanchemain (Paris, 1880), I, 16–20.
[36] *Ibid.*, I, 20–21. The love theme of Poliziano's "La Giostra" is partly
based on the love hunt. The hero Julio is overcome by Love while hunting the deer. "E con sue [Amore] man di leve aer compose/ La imagin
d'una cervia altera e bella,/ Con alta fronte, con corna ramose,/ Candida
tutta, leggiadretta e snella./ E come tra le fere paventose/ Al giovan
cacciator si offerse quella,/ Lieto spronò il destrier per lei seguire,/

The metaphor came into English poetry through Wyatt and
Shakespeare, and certainly explains the punning passage that
supplies a kind of comic relief at the end of the initial hymn.
"Said He, look how your Huntsman here/ Hath taught a
Faun to hunt his *Dear*."
   But the deer that is celebrated as it dies before our eyes,
the deer that the nymph associates not only with her own lost
love but also with her own death, is to be more closely defined than a plain, yet sometimes amusing, symbol of love. It
is a wounded deer, and as such it has a firm poetic ancestry,
because the theme which stems from the passage in the fourth
book of the *Aeneid* is introduced by Petrarch in sonnet CCIX.

> E qual cervo ferito di saetta,
> Col ferro avelenato dentr'al fianco,
> Fugge, e più duolsi quanto più s'affretta,
> Tal io con quello stral dal lato manco
> Che mi consuma e parte mi diletta,
> Di duol me struggo, e di fuggir me stanco.

The theme of the lover as a wounded deer was more particu-
larly worked out by Bembo in "Si come suol, poiche 'l verno
aspro e rio" [37] and given full voice by Ronsard in a sonnet that
makes Marvell's figure richer.

> Ainsi j'alloy sans espoir de dommage,
> Le jour qu'un oeil sur l'Avril de mon aage
> Tira d'un coup mille traits en mon flanc.[38]

   This first hymnlike section of "The Nymph" with its multi-
plicities of literary suggestion is succeeded by an expository
passage (25–70) wherein the φύσις (as the classical epicedists
would call it) of the fawn is delicately announced. The fawn

Pensando in brieve darle agro martíre" (*Le Stanze*, ed. Carducci [Bologna,
1912], p. 274).
   [37] *Gli Asolani e le Rime*, ed. Dionisotto-Casalone (Turin, 1932), p. 164.
   [38] *Œuvres*, ed. Vaganay (Paris, 1924), I, 73.

is affectionate; it is swift, deserving its normal ancient epithet
alipes; and it is whiter than a lady's hand. The almost heraldic
blending and contrasting of red and white that dye a large
portion of the remaining poem begin with, "I blusht to see its
foot more soft,/ And white." The nymph shares the colors of
the fawn, but the fawn is mainly important in that it is identified with the nymph, abandoned by her lover and condemned
to idleness and solitariness. Time is also stated for us; it is the
time that it takes to die, brief as the life of roses and lilies, of
weanling fawns, or of young girls betrayed in their innocence.

> But I am sure, for ought that I
> Could in so short a time espie,
> Thy Love was far more better then
> The love of false and cruel men.

The emphasis in the capital letter is not without value because
the fawn has become Love itself.

There is, however, a second hymn (71–91) that follows this
expository passage, and, by enlarging the memory of the past,
brings the poem to a peak of emotion. "I have a Garden of
my own" is a statement that doubles the sense of possession,
of loneliness, of inwardness. On the literal surface, the nymph
is the mistress of a real garden of roses and lilies where she
and the fawn joyed to be. But the garden is also a secret one,
the mind and the heart of the girl, where, in one sense, the
fawn played in the true spring. In another sense, while the
fawn lived "it was all, the Spring time of the years." A number
of critics have seen in Marvell's "The Garden" the symbol of
the human mind, and this garden has undoubtedly the same
intent. The garden of roses and lilies expresses the mind and
the nature of the weeping maid, and she communes in it and
through it with the fawn. Once again the tradition comes to
support this identification and interpretation.

To Plato the imaginative mind is like a garden, for the

Phaedrus informs us that it is in such a propitious plot that men of letters plant flowers for their pleasure.[39] In the *Ion*, poets are described as bringing songs culled in the gardens and glades of the Muses, "Μουσῶν κήπων," [40] a metaphor that Pindar also uses to describe his literary occupation: "χαρίτων νέμομαι κῆπον." [41] The *figura mentis* of the mind as a garden was staunchly supported by the fact that Epicurus taught in a garden and that his cult could be called "κηπολογος." The garden of Epicurus, says Cicero figuratively, was watered by the fountains of Democritus: "cuius Democriti fontibus Epicurus hortos suos inrigavit"; [42] and the hostile Seneca defined the Epicureans as "alienus hortulus." [43] The author of the *Ciris* begins with the same sort of poetic turn:

> Etsi me, vario iactatum laudis amore,
> Irritaque expertum fallacis praemia vulgi,
> Cecropius suavis exspirans hortulus auras
> Florentis viridi Sophiae complectitur umbra:
> Ut mens curet eo dignum sibi quaerere carmen. . . .

The garden is a classical equivalent of the mind; and it is not unfitting to find in this garden of roses and lilies the history of the nymph's inner life. We notice, too, that the fawn, the amorous substitute, becomes part of the girl's self and blends into the flowers with a sort of invisibility. It loses itself, a bank of lilies in "the flaxen Lillies shade"; a white thought in a white shade. It fills itself with roses, and laps its "virgin limbs" in "Whitest sheets of Lillies cold." Had it lived longer —the poet insists—it would have become an intrinsic part of the nymph's inward life.

[39] 276D.
[40] 534A.
[41] *Olymp.* IX.27.
[42] *De Nat. Deorum* I.120.
[43] *Epist.* IV.10.

Had it liv'd long, it would have been
Lillies without, Roses within.[44]

The *hortus mentis* is, then, the inner life of the girl, but it has other meanings, too, that make it congenial with the topic of the "cerf d'Amour."

According to Athenaeus,[45] the second Hieron of Syracuse had a garden in which he talked to men and which he called (if transliteration may be substituted for translation), "the Myth." The myth of the garden leads us toward another literary equivalent that helps to enrich the meaning of the metaphors in the nymph's place of retirement. It was in such a place of flowers, the *Symposium* [46] states, that Penia conceived Cupid by Poros; and the "Jardin d'Amour" tenanted by Eros and his mother during most of the Middle Ages comes immediately to mind. This "vergier clos" is not one of the wicked bowers of the enchantresses of the Italian romances; it is not Acrasia's garden. If we must find one like it, we could look at the symbolic garden of Alcinous, the sheltered orchard where spring reigns forever. In such a place, a nameless goliard who was Silvio's ancestor hunted girls when spring had allayed the cruelties of winter.

Dulcius est carpere
Iam lilium cum rosa
Dulcissimum est ludere
Cum virgine formosa.[47]

[44] Though it is outside the limits of poetic expression, it is interesting to notice that the early Fathers found reason in the Bible to regard the heart or the mind as a garden: see Tertullian, *Adversus Marcion*, ed. Kroymann (Vienna, 1906), pp. 524–25; Ambrose, *Opera*, ed, Schenkle (Vienna, 1902), III.362; St. Augustine, *In Joannes* (*PL*, XXXV, 1957).

[45] XII.542.

[46] 203B.

[47] *Carmina Burana* (Stuttgart, 1847), p. 181.

In a similar garden the disconsolate lover of *De Venus la Deesse d'Amour* is consoled and instructed in love.[48] After this time, the garden of loving delights spreads over a wide area and is filled with blossoms. It becomes in Italy the "Giardino d'Amore" where Poliziano's Julio wandered: "Veste la campagna/ Di rose, gigli, violette e fiori." [49] In France, it is known as the garden of love, which is painstakingly described by Jean Passerat.[50] It was also familiar to the English, for it is found in that wintered land in "Twicknam Garden" where the lover John Donne cries out in frozen desolation. The garden of the mind can be transformed by poetic music into the garden of love.

It is also plain that this garden was sown with two flowers, the lily and the rose, because the poets of Eros cannot speak of love without them.

> Rosa rubicundior
> Lilio candidior
> Omnibus formosior
> Semper in te glorior! [51]

The colors white and red suggest modesty and innocence, but both flowers possess the common implication of brevity, of the short lives of the nymph and her fawn. Valerius Flaccus supports this understanding when he compares the days of the lily to the flashing by of human life.

> Lilia per vernos lucent velut alba colores
> Praecipue, quis vita brevis totus que parumper
> Floret honor fuscis et iam Notus imminet alis.[52]

[48] Ed. Foerster (Bonn, 1880), p. 2.
[49] *La Giostra,* in *Le Stanze l'Orfeo e le Rime,* ed. Carducci (Bologna, 1912), pp. 299–316.
[50] *Œuvres,* ed. Blanchemain (Paris, 1880), I, 25–29.
[51] *Carmina Burana,* p. 208.
[52] VI.492–94.

In keeping with these verses, Horace, drinking in the company of friends, ponders the fate of the "breve lilium" and the tender rose.[53]

For the Latins and their cultural inheritors, the rose and the lily were symbols of youth, and of love and death in youth. The modest and anxious love of Lavinia is characterized by both flowers: "aut mixta rubent ubi lilia multa/ Alba rosa: talia virgo dabat ore colores"; [54] and to this we may join all of the sad commentary on the worldly rose that helped to annotate Herbert's rose poem. The flowers often appear in mediaeval poetry as kindred emblems. In the "De Rosae et Liliique Certamine" of Sedulius Scottus, we follow a debate between the rose and the lily that Spring, the arbiter, brings to a close when she urges the sister flowers to remember that they are signs of innocence, youth, death, virginity, and martyrdom.

> O rosa pulchra, tace; tua gloria claret in orbe;
> Regia sed nitidis dominentur lilia sceptris.
> Hinc decus et species vestrum vos laudat in aevum:
> Forma pudicitiae nostris rosa gliscat in hortis,
> Splendida Phebeo vos, lilia, crescite vultu;
> Tu, rosa, martyribus rutilam das stemmate palmam,
> Lilia, virgineas turbas decorate stolatas.[55]

As a consequence of this tradition, the Renaissance knew the history of the rose and lily and adorned its poetry with it.

The two flowers are wisely employed by Marvell in both their priestly and secular meanings. With their aid, he maintains the tones of innocence, youth, love, and death that make the partial chorus of the complaint. The sacred meaning of the garden, which Bradbrook, Lloyd Thomas, and William-

[53] I.36.16.
[54] *Aeneid* XII.68–69.
[55] *Opera*, ed. Traube, *PLAC* (Berlin, 1896), III, 230–31.

son have felt, is also present; yet it stays in a symbolic memory that surpasses the nearer echoes of the Psalms and the
Canticle. The nymph, who is a member of Diana's court and
also a young girl bewailing the loss of love, is something like
the weeping mother of Christ [56] just as she is, according to
Spitzer, something like Niobe. She is a mother of a dying creature that is at one and the same time her love (and since she
has created this passion, it is also herself) and the external
token of this love. All of this is a complicated literary truth
on phenomenal and numenal levels; but, essentially, she is not
a mother and the thing in which she believed has "proved
wild." For this reason, she is never quite certain of the token
itself: "his Gifts might be/ Perhaps as false or more than he."
The Virgin and Niobe are present in the same way that Christ
is present in the first hymn. They are associative metaphors;
they are not the poem.

The full union of Christian and pagan metaphors is found in
the final section of the poem. The fawn, while it dies as an
animal, becomes the "Saint" with whom its ancestors con-
sorted. Its medicinal tears, famous in the Renaissance pharma-
copoeia, are converted into relics for the shrine of the Virgin-
Diana. They are described in terms of the Biblical "holy

[56] The likeness of Diana to the Virgin is as obvious as the impious-pious
comparisons of Orpheus to Christ; moreover, thanks to Seznec (*La Sur-
vivance* [London, 1939], p. 233), we know that the comparison was made.
The Virgin, we also know, is the closed garden, the "hortus conclusus"
of Alanus de Insulis (*Anticlaudianus* [PL, CCX, 538]), or "le vergier clos"
of Guillaume of Normandy (R. Reinsch, "Les Joies Nostre Dame de Guillaume," *Zeitsch. für Roman. Phil.*, III [1879], 222). Her association with
the rose and the lily is everywhere in the Middle Ages and in the Roman
poetry of the Renaissance. "Tu es li lis où Diex repose;/ Tu es rosier qui
porte rose/ Blanche et vermeille," writes Rutebeuf (*Œuvres* [Paris, 1874],
II, 146); and John of Garland follows the same theme through part of the
Stella Maris (ed. Wilson [Cambridge, Mass., 1946], pp. 91, 121, 149). For
an unknown poet of the Merovingian age, the Virgin is "Lilium inter
spinas acutissimas" and "Rosa fulgentem castitatis robore" (*PLAC*, ed.
Winterfeld [Berlin, 1899], IV, 516–17).

frankincense," and at the same time they are associated with the pagan "electrum." The Heliades, whose brother was killed in his youth, are brought into the garden to weep with the nymph who has lost her fawn. The proper passage which levels the imaginative path to the completely static and sculptural finale is found in the place indicated by Marvell.

> nomenque in marmore lectum
> Perfudit lacrymis, et aperto pectore fovit.
> Nec minus Heliades fletus, et, inania morti
> Mundera, dant lacrymas.[57]

We are close to cepotaphic verse in these latter lines,[58] for the monument of the nymph and her fawn will mark their garden grave. The traditional statue of the fawn-loving Diana is similar to the Pietà, but it is not the same. The nymph realizes a satisfaction that she denied herself in life when she accepted a token and retreated to the garden. The fawn's affection, which might have passed, is now assured by its death. Love, which she found to be false in her one encounter with it in the real world; love, which was even uncertain in the garden, in the *hortis mentis,* is safe, unchanging, and everlasting only in the world of art. In this new world the nymph and the fawn are united eternally:

> but there
> Th' Engraver sure his Art may spare;

[57] Ovid *Metamorphoses* II.338–41. See also Hyginus 154; Claudian VII.125; XXVIII.165; Statius V.3.85–86; Martial IV.59.

[58] The ancient custom of garden burial is described by Tacitus (*Hist.* I.49.1) and Suetonius (*Galba* XX.2); for poetic records, see Ausonius CCXXXVIII; and Martial I.114. Since the previous critics of this poem have tried to assume that there is symbolism in the ermine, I can assure them that there is, although I do not think it is required. The ermine is associated with the lily as a symbol of purity and innocence in French literature from Marot's "De la Royne Claude," *Œuvres,* ed. Grenier (Paris, n.d.), II, 509 to St. Amant, *Œuvres,* ed. Livet (Paris, 1885), I, 300. One German minnesinger equated the ermine with Christ: see *Minnesinger,* ed. von der Hagen (Leipzig, 1838), II, 311.

For I so truly thee bemoane,
That I shall weep though I be Stone:
Until my Tears, still dropping, wear
My breast, themselves engraving there.

The flight from the realities of love to an ideal of love, Marvell seems to be saying, may be the course of caution, but even here the idea can be permanently fixed only by the hand of the artist. And yet the colors tell the story: whiteness alone remains; the red of sentient life is gone.

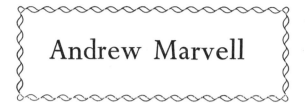

CHAPTER SEVEN

Andrew Marvell

"Upon Appleton House"

"Upon Appleton House" was written after Marvell had gone
to Nunappleton as tutor to Mary, the only child of the great
Lord Fairfax. It was a moment of retirement for both the poet
and his patron. Fairfax, who had led the armies against the
King, was appalled by the actions of the victorious Parliamen-
tarians. When the captive King was held for questioning, he
refused to sit with the committee of inquiry at Westminster.
Lady Fairfax, the "starry Vere," was present in the gallery and
spoke her mind in praise of her husband's absence and in con-
demnation of Cromwell. To her, the Captain of the Saints was
a traitor. General Fairfax was probably more controlled than
his wife; he remained with the army, assisting the government
in keeping the peace, until June, 1650. The occasion of his
retirement is noteworthy. The generals met to consider the in-
vasion of Scotland where rebellious troops were mustering;

Cromwell insisted that a preventive expedition was impera-
tive. The consultation, as Whitelocke records it, is solemn.
Fairfax saw no reason for the continuation of bloodshed; he
spoke out against it and resigned his command. "Every man
must stand or fall by his own conscience." [1] Marvell's stanza
XLV makes this honest conclusion into poetry.

> For he did, with his utmost Skill,
> *Ambition* weed, but *Conscience* till.
> *Conscience*, that Heaven-nursed Plant,
> Which most our Earthly Gardens want.
> A prickling leaf it bears, and such
> As that which shrinks at ev'ry touch;
> But Flowrs eternal, and divine,
> That in the Crowns of Saints do shine.

So Fairfax retired with his family to what his laureate called
in another poem "the happy Garden-state," leaving to those
of less conscience the "unweeded garden" of public life.

By seventeenth-century aristocratic standards, the place
to which they retreated was relatively modest.

> It was a picturesque brick mansion with stone copings and
> a high steep roof, and consisted of a centre and two wings at
> right angles, forming three sides of a square, facing to the north.
> The great hall or gallery occupied the centre between the two
> wings. It was fifty yards long, and was adorned with thirty
> shields of wood, painted with the arms of the family. In the
> three rooms there were chimney-pieces of delicate marble of
> various colours, and many fine portraits on the walls. The
> central part of the house was surrounded by a cupola, and
> clustering chimneys rose in the two wings. A noble park with
> splendid oak-trees, and containing 300 head of deer, stretched
> away to the north, while on the south side were ruins of the
> old Nunnery, the flower-garden, and the low meadows called
> *ings* extending to the banks of the Wharfe. In this flower-garden

---

[1] *Memorials* (Oxford, 1853), III, 207.

the General took especial delight. The flowers were planted in masses, tulips, pinks, and roses, each in separate beds, which were cut into the shape of forts with five bastions. General Lambert, whom Fairfax had reared as a soldier, also loved his flowers, and excelled both in cultivating them and in planting them from Nature. Lord Fairfax only went to Denton, the favorite seat of his grandfather, when the floods were out over the *ings* at Nunappleton, and he also occasionally resorted to his house at Bishop Hill in York.[2]

The prose account, written by Markham, who owned a lithograph no longer extant, supplies the poem with as many comments as the poem itself gives to the prose. In its way, it tells us no more than the poem, but the poem is really not about the house.

"Upon Appleton House" is a sequence of dramatic poems, skillfully divided, that celebrates the "house" in several ways. It is about the actual house, the actual gardens, fields, meadows, streams, and wood. It is about the house of Fairfax in past, present, and future. It is also about the house of flesh, the body and mind of man. The poem can be read as an ode in the manner of Pindar, for it not only praises Fairfax but also relates the necessary family myth, records the illustrious deeds, brings out the character of its subject, and phrases prophecies. The first ten stanzas are about the physical aspects of the house. It is architecturally British. No foreign architect vaulted (with Macbeth's notion of sprawling on the other side) "his brain" to produce it. As a consequence of this simplicity, the observer need not "arch the Brows" both in astonishment and in an optical effort to view it. "Vault" and "arch" are emphasized because the house contains, if Markham's print is correct, neither structural feature. The master builder abided, the poet then explains, by Nature's simple plan; he learned by the householding of bird, beast, and reptile

[2] *Life of the Great Lord Fairfax* (London, 1870), p. 365.

that one needs a house only slightly grander than oneself.
The third stanza of the description of the house proper is
based on the comparison, that had passed through many poetical fingers, of man's house of life to his tomb. Then, thinking
of the entrances to Norman keeps and seeing in them stony
symbols of the "needle's eye" of Matthew and Luke, Marvell,
like Gascoigne or some other Tudor conservative, recalls the
other England of Fairfax's great-grandfather.

> But all things are composed here
> Like Nature, orderly and near:
> In which we the Dimensions find
> Of that more sober Age and Mind,
> When larger sized Men did stoop
> To enter at a narrow loop;
> As practising, in doors so strait,
> To strain themselves through *Heavens Gate*.

The doctrine that true greatness is humbly expressed is illuminated by the examples of Romulus' "Bee-like Cell," the
humble "short but admirable lines" of Appleton House, and
the celebrated "homo perfectissimus" (the squared circle) of
Renaissance painting. In the ninth stanza we arrive before an
allegorical house not unlike Spenser's House of Holiness or
Alma's House; and at the end of this stanza, Marvell offers
a good poetical rendering of Fairfax's own bad lines, "Upon
the New-built House att Apleton."

> Thinke not o Man that dwells herein
> This House's a Stay but as an Inne
> Wch for Convenience fittly stands
> In way to one nott made with hands
> But if a time here thou take Rest
> Yett thinke Eternity's the Best.[3]

The tenth stanza adds this total description to the remainder
of the poem and provides us with a résumé of the topics that

[3] *The Poems*, ed. Reed (New Haven, Conn., 1909), p. 279.

will be poetically discussed: "fragrant Gardens, shaddy Woods,/ Deep Meadows, and transparent Floods."

The topics thus stated, topics that really weave the whole poem together and make a theme for the ultimate section on Mary Fairfax, are suppressed for twenty-five paragraphs while Marvell, directing our eyes toward the ruins of the nunnery, recites the legend of the family, satirizes the conventual life, provides his retired patron with an example of action in difficult times and circumstances, and sweeps the way for his eventual celebration of his charge, Mary Fairfax. We then leave the past and pass into the present garden, which is both the prelapsarian state and ante-bellum England. The garden's security enables us to view from afar the fields and water meadows in which is enacted an allegorical masque of the recent civil disorders. With stanza LXI, Marvell's personal *Apologia pro Vita Sua* begins as he forsakes history and biography for autobiography. The last poem is written in praise of the house in the person of its twelve-year-old heiress. Here we sense something similar to Donne's *Anniversaries*. The poem is, then, a group of poems on a central subject like those that Marvell wrote about the Mower. It has a place, as most Renaissance poems do, in a long poetic history.

Poems about great men and their houses begin with Homer's description of the palace and gardens of King Alcinous. It is to this house that Athena leads Odysseus when he is stranded on the Phaeacian shores. Bronze, the metal of the house—the hardest known to men of Hesiod's Third Age— symbolizes the qualities of both the king and his realm. But strength and solidity alone do not make a kingdom, so Odysseus has hardly reached the threshold before splendor assails his eyes. The blaze that almost confounds him and that fills the long hall is that of the sun and moon: "ὥστε γὰρ ἠελίου αἴγλη πέλεν ἠὲ σελήνης."[4] Opposites, as the Greeks understood them, embrace in this metaphor and time and space are

[4] VII.84.

Homerically cancelled. It is, however, only fiction that insists on the presence of the sun and moon in the hall; for it is their mundane representatives, gold and silver, that produce the illusion in the fire-shine. The two metals are everywhere. The doorposts and lintel are silver; the doorhook is gold. Pairs of silver and gold dogs, fashioned by the skill of Hephaestus, guard the house of the "great-hearted one" from death and keep it forever ageless.[5] The fact that time, even seasonal change, avoids the house is symbolically suggested by youths of gold who light the hall with torches.

Without are the gardens, the first and fairest in the history of man. Here nature lives and prospers under the true light of the sun and moon, but now the light and heat are divinely ordained. No dogs of precious metal protect the gardens; no figures of youthful firmness hold torches there. "Such are also the splendid gifts of the gods" that the gardens are beyond the rage of earthly time. Age and Death are divinely fended off. "Of these never does the fruit decay or fail, winter or summer, lasting through the year."[6] Solidity, endurance, timelessness, and eternity—qualities uncharacteristic of Odysseus' experiences before Troy and on the weary homeward voyage—are summarized in King Alcinous and expressed poetically by his house and gardens. It is small wonder then that he is named "Ἀλκι + νοος" (strength of mind) and that he is wisely married to Arete or "excellence."

The house and gardens of Alcinous are both real and ideal. They represent the habitation of a great magnate of a Greek kingdom; on the other hand, they stand for high qualities of character, for mental force. In these respects they are not unlike the "castellum mentis," the Acropolis of Plato,[7] and the "Arx" of Cicero;[8] the single strongholds in a failing world.

[5] VII.94.
[6] VII.117–18.
[7] Republic 560B.
[8] De Natura Deorum II.140.

Though the Greeks do not want for descriptive poetry about public buildings, there is, I think, no other poetical description of a royal abode like that of Alcinous, which supplies us with both a literal and a moral reading. The Middle Ages followed the moral sense when it erected the poetical structures, palaces and gardens, that housed and entertained its massive personifications; and from the mediaeval blueprints, the poets of the *romanzi* drew the details for the residences of their thinly clad creatures of vice and virtue. This is the tradition that eventuates in the allegorical houses of the *Faerie Queene*. I shall not pretend that Homer had anything to do with the fabrication of the tradition that the Middle Ages and Renaissance followed. The bridge between the house of Alcinous and that of Lord Fairfax is anchored on an Italian pier, because it was the Romans, rather than the Greeks who emphasized the private house as the expression of the character and biography of the great man. For them the villa was autobiography; whereas the tomb, scarred over with flattery, was the work of a hired biographer.

With his descriptions of the houses of Dido and Latinus, Vergil follows the direction of Homer, but the most allegorical house erected by an early Latin poet is the Palace of Pelops which appears in Seneca's *Thyestes*. This house is the moral antithesis of the palace of Alcinous. It stands on a high place and faces south; its halls gleam with many colors; but it is environed with desperation and death. Planted to yew and cypress, its garden is without sun, and through it flows a dismal stream, which gathers in black pools and is filled with the voices of the dead. There is fire but it provokes no metaphors of light; it blazes in a savage wood and reveals horror.

> Quidquid audire est metus
> Illic videtur; errat antiquis vetus
> Emissa bustis turba et insultant loco
> Maiora notis monstra; quin tota solet
> Micare silva flamma, et excelsae trabes

Ardent sine igne. Saepe latratu nemus
Trino remugit, saepe simulacris domus
Attonita magnis. Nec dies sedat metum;
Nox propria luco est et superstitio inferum
In luce media regnat.[9]

The House of Pelops knocks at the gate of allegory, but it
is also as real as its fate. Homer in his description of the palace
of Alcinous feathered over the moral with the literal reading;
in Seneca it is the second meaning that makes the surface
sheen. By placing the two texts together, we have the cross and
pile, the two faces of the coin of symbolism. Yet it is Statius,
rather than Homer or Seneca, who truly makes the die of the
mode that later poets followed when they praised a man by
describing his house.

   In the epithalamium that he wrote for the marriage of Ar-
runtius Stella and Violantilla, Statius describes the bride's
house in Rome.[10] The description is full but not independent,
for it is part of the marriage hymn, a piece of scenic enamel
in the plaque of celebration. In two other poems of the *Silvae*,
one on the Tiberine villa of Manilius Vopiscus and another on
the villa of Pollus Felix at Sorrento, the poet makes house and
gardens describe their master. The first villa stands on both
banks of the Anio and is surrounded by forest; it is the emblem, consequently, of coolness and quiet. It is richly adorned;
but in contrast to things fashioned by men, Nature supplies
her final elaborations, sending a stream through every room
and a great tree through the roof. Calm, shade, temperateness
rule in the house and its yards, proclaiming that its master is
both a philosopher and a poet.[11] In contrast, the verses on the
villa at Sorrento exalt the qualities of beauty and self-content.
Like Lord and Lady Fairfax, Pollius and his wife have retired

[9] 670–79.
[10] *Silvae* I.2.140–60.
[11] I.3.

from the city with its hordes of ambitious people. Important once in the affairs of state, the master has withdrawn from public life in order to devote himself to permanent things. He is worthy, says Statius, of the peace and beauty that surround him. "Ite per annos/ Saeculaque et priscae titulos praecedite famae." [12]

Martial, the contemporary of Statius, takes over the mode in his comparison of Faustinus' villa near Baiae with Bassus' house at Rome,[13] setting, so literary historians have said, the pattern for English poems on country houses. His poem actually is somewhat outside of the tradition, for it is essentially a satire on the great villas in the imperial city. It certainly gave Browning the idea for "Up at a Villa"; but for the poets of the seventeenth century, the descriptions of Statius are far more suggestive. I think that this conjecture is reasonable because Statius stands behind the descriptive poems of the fourth century Bishop Sidonius, whose verses on the house of Pontius Leontius are the most fitting precursor of "Upon Appleton House."

The "Burgus Pontii Leontii" begins with a description of the natural location of the house; then a myth, similar to Marvell's nunnery legend, is told. Dionysus and Apollo meet and lament the desecration of their rites in Greece. Apollo proposes that they join powers and found a common shrine at the confluence of the Dordogne and Garonne. Gifted with foresight, the god describes the house that Paulinus Pontius, the founder of the line, will raise on this place and the illustrious race that there will be bred. Situated on a summit, the house will display two towers, signifying "splendor and aid." Its doorstone will be a memorial of celebrated names; its walls will shine with painting and sculpture. The eyes of Apollo-Sidonius, like those of Marvell, leave the house and wander

[12] II.2.145–46.
[13] III.58

over its cool colonnades, granaries, baths, gardens, fields, streams, and waterfall. The house speaks for the characters of its founders, but chiefly proclaims the greatness of Pontius and his wife, "than whom no other lady of the Pontian house ever rejoiced more in her husband's illustrious career." [14] In this house, the poet Sidonius was received and his poem about the retired Leontius, "easily the first of the men of Aquitaine," is very much like Marvell's poem on the house of the General who had left the service of the state.

The great house as the mirror of its owner is the subject of various continental poems [15] prior to those written by Jonson, Carew, and Marvell; but these English poems surpass their continental predecessors in skill and merit. There is no question that Marvell's poem is superior in its generation because of its hidden complications and its blending of traditions. But this can only be shown by explanation, and so I shall leave Nunappleton and follow Marvell into the garden.

The garden of Appleton House is not the garden of "The Garden" or the garden in which the Nymph, withdrawn from life, sported with her white fawn. This is a new garden, the work of a poet-gardener, who sees to it that we understand its meaning. In stanza XLI, Marvell tells us flatly that the place through which we saunter with Lord and Lady Fairfax is England. It is not the England of 1650, but the England of earlier years, not unlike the "hortus amoenissimus" of Adam and Eve. There is, however, a difference; the garden has not been corrupted by sin. It is the outside world that has fallen.

[14] *Carmina* XXII.

[15] See Lorenzo Gambara's "Arcis Caprarolae Descriptio," in *Poemata* (Antwerp, 1579), pp. 3–37; Marcantonio Flaminio's "Ad Villam Mariam," in *Carmina Quinque Illustrium Poetarum* (Florence, 1552), pp. 136–37; Francisco Berni's "In Descrizione della sua Casa," *Le Rime*, ed. Palazzi (Genoa, 1915), pp. 150–52; Théophile's "La Maison de Sylvie," *Œuvres*, ed. Alleaume (Paris, 1855), II, 193–230; Tristran l'Hermite's "La Maison d'Astrée," in *Les Amours*, ed. Camo (Paris, 1925), pp. 244–55. Jonson's "Penshurst" and Carew's "Saxham House" make up the English count.

The theme seems to be an elaboration of the notion that, had our first parents stood, they would have remained in the garden; but even then Cain, the founder of cities, would have brought sin to mankind. We do not need Marvell to tell us that the English state is a garden, for Shakespeare anticipated him in *II Henry VI, Richard II,* and *Henry V.* Old Gaunt knew that England was another Eden; but who told him?

There is, first, a Hebraic answer to the question asked by this metaphor. Besides the Garden of Eden, there was Solomon's maze of roses, lilies, and palms that fixed the Queen of Sheba in admiration and supplied the *mise en scène* for the Canticle. St. John tells us that Mary Magdalene mistook her risen Lord for the "hortulanus" of the garden; and if Christ-Pastor can become the shepherd-king, the king can be a gardener. To these figures can be added those supplied by the pagans. Semiramis, Cyrus, and Epicurus were garden-makers; Caesar willed his gardens to the Romans; and Scipio, Lucullus, Augustus, and Diocletian retired to cultivate their flowers. But the poetic connection between statecraft and gardening is made by associations beyond those of the Bible, history, and mythology.

For the ordinary Roman, the gardens that covered Italy had symbolic meaning; they represented the status of their masters and were microcosms of the Roman Empire. Vitruvius makes it clear that a garden was an aristocratic requirement, "suitable to their consummate majesty," "ad decorum maiestatis perfectae." [16] The significance of the garden as something beyond the hopes of an ordinary citizen is tacitly expressed by Cato and Varro in their books on agriculture. To make this point openly, Columella puts his book on gardening into verse. Even Vergil, who uses hexameters for his four books on agriculture, admits that gardening is beyond the limits of his poem and leaves it as a special subject for others. "Verum haec ipse

[16] VI.7.10.

equidem spatiis exclusus iniquis/ Praetereo atque aliis post me
memoranda relinquo."

If the texts may be credited, the Roman aristocrat attempted
to recreate the Roman world within the walls of urban gardens. Chrysippus, according to Plutarch, complained about
the nobles who made their gardens into representations of
the great world,[17] and Seneca the Rhetorician reports the
speech of the lawyer Fabianus Papirius against this practice.[18]
To these "Stoics Against the Gardens" one can add Pliny's
account of the attempt to show the real world in the yard of
a villa through the services of a "topiarius" [19]—a word made
from *topia*, a "landscape painting." He describes the "pic-
turae" and "imagines rerum" [20] that filled these open places
and, then, the more specific Vitruvius tells us about "the ports,
promontories, shores, rivers, fountains, temples, mountains,
herds, and even shepherds" fashioned by the "topiarius." [21]
So all of Nature and the Roman world were brought within
these narrow limits and irrigated by streams to which one gave
names like "Nile" [22] or "Euripus." [23] The little Syrian of the
"Copa," a poem we can hope is Vergil's, gives us a charming
verse description of a garden.

> Sunt topia et kalybae, cyathi, rosa, tibia, chordae,
>   Et triclia umbrosis frigida harundinibus.
> En et Maenalio quae garrit dulce sub antro
>   Rustica pastoris fistula in ore sonat.
> Est et vappa, cado nuper defusa picato,
>   Et strepitans rauco murmure rivus aquae.
> Sunt et cum croceo violae de flore corollae

[17] *De Stoicorum Repugnantibus* 21.
[18] *Controversariae* II.1.10.
[19] *Naturalis Historia* IV.29; XII.22; XVI.76, 140; XVIII.242.
[20] XVI.140.
[21] VII.5.
[22] Cicero *Ad Quintum* III.9.
[23] Statius, I.3.31.

Sertaque purpurea lutea mixta rosa
Et quae virgineo libata Achelois ab amne
Lilia vimineis attulit in calathis.[24]

The garden, as Marvell certainly knew, was associated with kings and brightened with Christian meaning. Whether he understood its representational qualities as the Romans saw them I do not know; he had lately been in Rome and he cannot have missed its floral splendors. At any rate it is clear from explicit statement that the garden at Nunappleton is also a symbol of the state. It is, however, more than this, for Marvell plainly tells us that it is a garrison. Its planter was a man of warlike exploits, and the first baron was also a man to make flowery jests.

Who, when retired here to Peace,
His warlike Studies could not cease;
But laid these Gardens out in sport
In the just Figure of a Fort;
And with five Bastions it did fence,
As aiming one for ev'ry Sense.

When we follow Lord Fairfax through the garden, we are really attending a review. The flowers let "fragrant Vollyes" fly, and like regiments on parade "Under their *Colours* stand displaid." But the garden which is the state and the citadel of state is more specifically defined.

This is one of the least particularized of all gardens; it pales before those of the late Greek romances; [25] Perdita's garden is a Luxembourg compared to it; "The Garden" could give instruction to its planter. It contains only three kinds of flowers; it has no birds, for they and the butterflies have fled to the wood where Marvell will write his life story. The

[24] 7–16.
[25] See Achilles Tatius *De Clitophontis et Leucippes Amoribus* I.15; and Longus *De Daphnide et Chloe* II.3.

only living creature in the garden besides the poet, the Fairfax family, and us is the bee. The bee hums through "these known Allies"; he sounds reveille, "Beating the *Dian* with its *Drumms*," to awaken the flowers; he stands watch at night.

> Then in some Flow'rs beloved Hut
> Each Bee as Sentinel is shut;
> And sleeps so too: but, if once stir'd,
> She runs you through, or askes *the Word*.

The bee is governor of the garden; the rose, the tulip, the dianthus are the garrison troops.

It is not hard to understand why the bee dominates a garden which represents an ideal state. The fourth book of the *Georgics*, the Book of the Bee, is a poem on beekeeping and an account of an ideal commonwealth. Bees, Vergil tells us, live under the majesty of the law. They divide the labors of state by covenant. The older bees have charge of the towns, of hive-building, of making the well-wrought house. The young work in the fields and bring the harvest home. They are devoted to their king. While he is secure, they are of one mind; when he is lost, they destroy everything. The king is the guardian of their toils and they do him reverence. They stand round him in crowds, attend him in throngs, carry him on their shoulders. "For him they expose their bodies to battle and seek death through glorious wounds." They do all this because they have a share of the divine intelligence.

> His quidam signis atque haec exempla secuti
> Esse apibus partem divinae mentis et haustus
> Atherios dixere.[26]

Vergil saw in the government of bees what the Greeks had seen and what others were to see again and again. The hive

[26] 219–21.

is an ideal state of ordered ranks governed by a king. The bee alone inhabits Marvell's garden because it is the ideal England, the fortress Eden shut off from the rest of the world by the "watry . . . Sword" of the first of the "four Seas." This passage probably records the disordered realm. The great Lord was too tender in mind to endure any government except the best. His poetic companion, the old Corycian who had a garden near Tarentum, the city of Pythagoras, also appears in Vergil's fourth *Georgic*. Here in a land unfit for the plough and the flock, unkind to the vine, the old gardener grew the white lily, vervain, roses, apples, pears, plums, hyacinths, and limes. His garden, too, rang with the hum of bees and so, says Vergil, he equalled in contentment the wealth of kings. "Regum aequabat opes animis." [27] The episode in the Latin poem symbolizes a higher existence, a turning away from the harshness of the world to make a park of flowers near the city of the philosophers. In his concluding stanza, Marvell almost says the same.

> And yet their walks one on the Sod
> Who, had it pleased him and *God*,
> Might once have made our Gardens spring
> Fresh as his own and flourishing.
> But he preferr'd to the *Cinque Ports*
> These five imaginary Forts:
> And, in those half-dry Trenches, spann'd
> Pow'r which the Ocean might command.

We now leave the ideal state of the garden to visit the fields and the water meadows, where we shall see "how Chance's better Wit/ Could with a Mask my studies hit." The masque that we shall watch will be one of war and social chaos.

The sequence of stanzas (XLVII–LXI) that describes the harvest and the flood, when "*Denton* sets ope its *Cataracts*,"

[27] 125–48.

must be first read as a literal record. These things Marvell saw
and transmuted into poetical allegories. He saw men dive
into the long corn and bring up flowers that grew between
the furrows, and he thought of those who dived for pearl and
sponge. Then the waving grain became a great green sea, and
the reapers who fought its currents became Jews fleeing from
the hosts of Pharoah. This story touched off the memories of
quail and manna, of the time when the rails died under
the scythemen's strokes. The harvest dances, the flood in the
meadow, the stranded cattle were all literal pictures stored in
the gallery of his mind. They hung there, like those of Clora,
ready to be transferred to canvas or plaster by Lely or the
Davenant artist; and Marvell mentions these painters so that
we can know these scenes are first to be understood as real.

Marvell's main purpose is not to construct a panorama.
There is more to see in this landscape than fifty acres of
country life, and Marvell forces us to see it by a series of
blunt suggestions. The grass is massacred; the low-nesting rail
is slain; the field is transformed into "A Camp of Battail
newly fought"; the mowers change into "Victors" and,
covered with "*Alexanders sweat*," they dance "Triumphs."
The flood in the water meadow is, of course, also the Flood
that destroyed the antediluvian giants, the one from which
"the first Carpenter" escaped in his Ark. The "Toril" at
Madrid is "rase and pure" "ere the Bulls enter," but it is
shortly disarrayed and bloodied. The reference to the "Levellers" in stanza LVII is direct, and the concluding stanza (LX)
is so in the tradition of a Merlin or Nostradamus that we cannot avoid the political implications of the whole section.

The opening scene in the fields is traditionally pastoral,
but like its pattern, the *Eclogues* of Vergil, it means more
than it says. War, as Marvell and we know, is a harvest and
the soldier is a reaper under the master mower, Death. The
metaphor of the soldier-reaper first appeared in the *Argo-*

nautica of Apollonius of Rhodes when Jason, "hastening to make harvest of the sons of earth," is compared to a farmer who rushes out to gather his unripe grain at the approach of an army."[28] The metaphor is extended to all forms of hand-to-hand combat. Aeneas mows down lines of men as he seeks out Turnus: "Proxima quaeque metit gladis latumque per agmen/ Ardens limitem agit ferro, te, Turne, superbum/ Caede nova quaerens."[29] The *Punica* of Silius Italicus makes the same comparison over and over: "metit agmina" (IV. 462), "ense metit rapido" (X. 146), "est oblatum metit insatiabilis agmen" (XIII. 218), "gregem metite imbellem" (XIV. 134), "hanc segetem mete" (XVI. 615). The war-harvesting metaphor is widespread but one of the most striking classical references—the great hero, reaping soldiers as a mower cuts the grain—appears in a fourth-century epic, the *Johannidos*.

> Armipotens, hostes cernens obstare, Johannes
> Irruit in densas acies, turmasque rebelles
> Letifero mucrone secat, ceu messor acuta
> Falce metit segetes maturo tempore sollers;
> Et modo cum teneris culmos compressat aristis
> Laeva manus, nunc dextra secat, nunc fune tenaci
> Colligat innumeros gaudens per rura maniplos.[30]

To the metaphors of classical antiquity we must add those of Christian provenance, the reaping angel of The Revelation [31] and the scriptural comparison of man to grass.[32] The figure is now a cliché, but it was fresh enough for Marvell when he made it into allegory.

The metaphor of war as harvest is linked in the poetry of Horace with the companion metaphor of civil war as flood.

---

[28] III.1386–90.
[29] X.513–15.
[30] Ed. Partsch (Berlin, 1878), VIII, 534–40.
[31] 14:14–19.
[32] Isaiah 40:6; Psalms 90:6, 102:12; Job 5:26, 14:2; I Peter 1:24.

In the fourteenth ode of Book IV, inundation, reaping, and the bull, though not at Madrid, are garnered in a series of verses.

> Sic tauriformis volvitur Aufidus,
> Qui regna Dauni praefluit Apuli,
>   Cum saevit horrendamque cultis
>   Diluviem meditatur agris,
>
> Ut barbarorum Claudius agmina
> Ferrata vasto diruit impetu,
>   Primosque et extremos metendo
>   Stravit humum. . . . .

The flood metaphor of this poem really begins with the fifth book of the *Iliad* where Tydeides is described as storming "across the field like a winter stream in flood, scattering the barriers; the long lines of dikes cannot hold it in, nor the fences of fruitful orchards stop its sudden rush when the rains drive it; and the works of the sons of men perish in multitudes before it." [33] Sophocles [34] and Aeschylus [35] use the same image for war, and in due course the Latins have it too. Aeneas rages across the fields like a torrent of black water; [36] the heroic Fabian gens marches down into the valley like a river over its banks. [37] Sempronius, a hero of the *Punica*, rides into the foe like a torrent falling from Pindus and racing across the fields; [38] and elsewhere in the same poem, the Romans sweep all before them like a flood while Hannibal, forlorn in hope, observes the destruction. [39]

In Latin poetry the metaphor of the flood becomes special-

---

[33] V.87–91.
[34] *Antigone* 129.
[35] *Persians* 87–89, 412; *Seven* 1067–70.
[36] X.602.
[37] Ovid *Fasti* II.219–23.
[38] IV.520–23; XVII.121–24.
[39] XII.184–90.

ized as a symbol of internecine conflict. It was an inundation of the Eridanus, says Vergil, that preceded the Battle of Philippi:

> Proluit insano contorquens vertice silvas
> Fluviorum rex Eridanus camposque per omnis
> Cum stabulis armenta tulit.[40]

Horace, urging the Romans to accept Augustus and avoid civil war, uses the same topic in his second ode. Shall we, he asks, let the awful age of Proteus return when fish flounder in tree-top nests, when deer swim panic-stricken "through plain heaped on plain."

> Vidimus flavom Tiberim retortis
> Litore Etrusco violenter undis
> Ire deiectum monimenta regis
>   Templaque Vestae,
>
> Iliae dum se nimium querenti
> Iactat ultorem, vagus et sinistra
> Labitur ripa Iove non probante u-
>   xorius amnis.

To assure us that floods and civil wars are the same, Lucan prefaces his epic of the great internal struggle for power with the same trope: "Tethys maioribus undis/ Hesperiam Calpen summumque implevit Atlanta." [41]

The metaphors of harvest and flood make it plain that this portion of "Upon Appleton House" is concerned with war and civil disturbance. History has torn up the garden in which the royal bee presided and where the flowers marched in orderly regiments. The "sweet Militia" of rose and tulip, reminding us of Dante's "In forma dunque di candida rosa/ Mi si mostrava la milizia santa," [42] is dispersed and only the

[40] *Georgics* I.481–83.
[41] *Pharsalia* I.554–55.
[42] *Paradiso* XXXI.1–2.

sensitive flower of conscience that adorns the heavenly crown of Fairfax is left. There are flowers among the corn, but man must dive for them as for sunken treasure. Shortly these flowers, wild and unvalued by the gardener, will be reaped with the grain or strangled in the flood.

Poetry about mowers and harvest is usually in the pastoral vein; but what a bitter pastoralism this is. Under a rural disguise the war against the King is fought in rime. The first word to be capitalized is "Abyss," the "barathrum" of increate nature, of unspeakable depth. The grass of man's flesh makes the substance of the chaos, but men "like Grasshoppers appear,/ But Grasshoppers are Gyants there." At first sight, the image is excitingly natural, for the insects on the "green spir's" are taller than the grass-men wading in the sea-green vortex. The grasshoppers of this battle piece have been identified [43] with the grasshopper metaphor in Numbers: [44] "And there we saw the giants, the sons of Anak, which come of the giants: and we were in our own sight as grasshoppers, and so we were in their sight"; but the Biblical quotation that explains this more clearly is in Nahum: "Thy crowned are as the locusts, and thy captains as the great grasshoppers, which camp in the hedges in the cold day, but when the sun ariseth they flee away, and their place is not known where they are." [45] The English insect has a Hebrew history.

Perhaps we must think of these grasshoppers, as Lovelace does,[46] as soldiers and as kingly ones. It is not by chance that the mowers follow them, destroying their food and refuge, and laying the fields more bare than ever. Nicander, one of the earliest of Greek poets, describes the grasshopper army,

---

[43] Joan Grundy, "Marvell's Grasshoppers," *N & Q* (N.S. IV, 1957), p. 142; see Pierre Legouis' reply and announcement of his earlier notice in *N & Q* (N.S. V, 1958), pp. 108–109.

[44] 13:33.

[45] 3:17.

[46] See Chapter Five.

its troops with wing-sedged backs, flying over the crops, eating the grain, and wasting the fields as with fire.[47] What seem first to have been allied in analogy by this poet become in time commonplace, and Alciati makes the insects symbolic for the Renaissance in his emblem, "Nil Reliqui," through which the grasshopper and the armies of Atilla and Xerxes are made figuratively the same.

> Scilicet hoc deerat post tota mala, denique nostris
> Locustae ut raperent quicquid inesset agris.
> Vidimus innumeras Euro duce tendere turmas,
> Qualia non Atylae, castrave Xerxes erant.[48]

The reign of the royal grasshoppers is short as the day, for their human counterparts, the parliamentary mowers, dramatically "enter next" and take their place in the masque. They are the "Israelites," God's chosen wasters who, after the plagues of frogs, lice, flies, and grasshoppers were ended, spoiled their Egyptian masters. One member of their party, the shepherdess Thestylis, now a cruel *vivandière*, is pointed out for our careful contemplation.

> But bloody *Thestylis*, that waites
> To bring the mowing Camp their Cates,
> Greedy as Kites has thrust it up,
> And forthwith means on it to sup:
> When on another quick She lights,
> And cryes, he call'd us *Israelites;*
> But now, to make his saying true,
> Rails rain for Quails, for Manna Dew.

The Hebraic allusions in these lines are explained by Genesis 32:28, where we read how the name of Jacob was changed to Israel, and by the sixteenth chapter of Exodus with its account of the miracles of quails and manna. Be-

---

[47] *Theriaca* 801–803.
[48] *Emblemata* (Paris, 1580), p. 469.

hind the Bible is Bible-quoting Cromwell, who, like a true
Puritan, regularly referred to his adherents in speech and
letter as "the People of God," an English translation of
"Israelites." After the victory at Marston Moor, the Captain
of the Saints anticipated Marvell's mowers when he wrote to
a friend: "God made them as stubble to our swords." So
Thestylis, queen of "The Women that with forks it fling"
who "represent the Pillaging," has both God and God's vice-
roy, the commander of "the Godly Party," in mind. Though
there is some slight connection between this shepherdess
and Deborah or Jael, she really comes from pagan antiquity
to make Marvell's bloody point.

Thestylis is not a very close relative of the girl who helps
Theocritus' Simaetha brew a love philter; she is better related
to Vergil's Thestylis, who grinds garlic and thyme for the
field laborers and who covets Corydon's roes, but she belongs
to the left side of the family. This girl is really more of a man
than the mowers, because as one of them recoils from his
inadvertent murder of the rail, she "thrusts up" the slain bird
and takes a live one (wringing its neck I suppose) from a nest.
The epithet that is attached to her is "bloody," and this adjective enables us to recognize her as the sister or wife of
Mars, "sanguinea Bellona." [49]

In Thestylis, the warlike amazon of antiquity is given
pastoral dress and placed at the exact center of the masque
of war; so her past is concealed while it is simultaneously
revealed. Vergil knew her as she wandered, bloody scourge
in hand, through the fields of war: "Quam cum sanguineo
sequitur Bellona flagello." [50] Silius Italicus discovers her with
gore-drenched hair among the fighting men; [51] and as Lucan
points out, she is always eager for more slaughter. In her

---

[49] Statius *Thebiados* IX.297.
[50] *Aeneid* VIII.703.
[51] V.220–21.

honor, the flamens slice their limbs and drink goblets of blood: "Tum quos sectis, Bellona lacertis/ Saeva movet, cecinere deos, crinemque rotantes/ Sanguinem." [52] She moves through the centuries, maddening soldiers with blood-lust and swinging her reddened lash. Most war poems mention her, and Shakespeare, we remember, calls Macbeth that "man of blood," "Bellona's bridegroom." For Marvell she represents the excesses that a long war brings, even when it is a war fought for principles and conducted by Christians. The history of Fairfax's horror at the King's execution (the slaughtered rail?) and his refusal to attack Scotland (the quick rail?) is possibly given a share in this poetic masque.

It is clear that the rails have political meaning, and that they also contain a lesson for both Fairfax and Marvell. As far as I know, the bird appears in these verses for the first time in a poetic context; but Marvell certainly knew that the "rallus crex" was known to the Italians as "re di quaglie" and to the French as "roi des cailles." The bird is the king of quail, though not a quail itself; hence God, who sent the quails to the hungry Israelites, now rains kings into the laps of the British Jews. The bird is also neutral. It is sometimes a wading bird and sometimes it comes to the fields and lives with the quails. It is difficult to classify.[53]

With the emphatic "Unhappy Birds!" of stanza LII, Marvell ponders the question of neutrality (his personal problem), and the question of retirement (Fairfax's problem). A question often posed by disturbed men through scores of centuries is also phrased implicitly: "Is there any place in which man is safe from disaster?" The general question provides a kind of text for the sermon to the rails: "To build below the Grasses Root;/ When Lowness is unsafe as Hight,/ And Chance o'retakes what scapeth spight." One must build

[52] I.565–67.
[53] U. Aldrovandus, *Ornithologia* (Bologna, 1637), III, 455–56.

so high, says Marvell ironically, that one is out of danger, or
one must be born early enough to be safely dead when
disaster occurs. "Or sooner hatch or higher build." Both
courses are clearly impossible. Marvell has heard the "Orphan
Parents" of many a dead man on each side of the conflict
lament the necessity of taking sides; but there is no salvation
in neutrality as the fate of the water and land rails proves.
"Neuters," said the Roundhead committees, "deserve neither
respect nor protection from Church or Commonwealth"; and
their decision was seconded by the clergy, preaching on a
text from the victory song of Deborah: "Curse ye Meroz,
said the angel of the Lord, curse ye bitterly the inhabitants
thereof; because they came not to the help of the Lord, to
the help of the Lord against the mighty." [54] The King's men
joined their opponents in their scorn and persecution of the
lukewarm attitude.

With stanza LIII the allegory of the Civil Wars ends.
The harvest is stacked, the reapers dance for the death of
the corn and for their victory. The green sea goes, leaving a
shoal of dangerous rocks or a desert as bare as the Sahara.
Death is present in the pyramids of Memphis or the Roman
funeral mounds. True enough, these are only hayricks, but
the poet's eye sees them as tombs. They are memorials of
"Soldiers Obsequies," but the trouble is not over, a few more
men must die. The flood spreads over the meadows, conflict
begins within the Parilamentary ranks.

The last forty lines of the war section of the poem may
have something to do with the Leveller Movement, and
especially with the political events of the spring of 1649.
The "Scene," which we are asked to observe, because, of
course, we are still at the masque, is "A levell'd space." It
is a flat canvas, the Toril, the world before the Flood, a

[54] Judges 5:23; see G. M. Trevelyan, England under the Stuarts (London,
1926), pp. 226–27.

"naked equal Flat/ Which *Levellers* take Pattern at." This is all in the open, but there are allusions that are hidden from us. In stanza LVI, Marvell writes "The World when first created sure/ Was such a Table rase and pure," and we hear the Diggers singing, "And then we shall see/ Brave Community,/ When Vallies lye levell with Mountaines." [55] If we have missed the point, Marvell refers us to Davenant's *Gondibert* and almost gives us a page reference.

> The strait an universal Herd appears;
> First gazing on each other in the shade;
> Wondring with *levell'd* Eies, and lifted Ears,
> Then play, whilst yet their Tyrant is unmade.[56]

The history of the Leveller Movement and of its splinter party, the Diggers, is well known.[57] Marvell, however, was so close to the whole eruption that he probably did not distinguish between the aims of the two groups. Fairfax was deeply involved in the attempt to suppress both parties, and the spring of 1649, when the winter's thaw enabled Denton to set "ope its *Cataracts*," the flood of rebellion occurred. By decisive action Fairfax smashed the mutiny at Burford. The tone of rebellion is supplied too by the last stanza (LX), which looks toward "Nostradamus Prophecy" and repeats in different form the tropes of Horace's poem on the Roman revolution: eels in oxen, leeches on horses, boats over bridges, fish in stables. It is all another way of saying, valleys as high as mountains. Fairfax's service to the state has now been poetically glossed, and Marvell has suggested to him that

[55] G. Winstanley, *The Works*, ed. Sabine (Ithaca, N. Y., 1941), p. 659.

[56] *Gondibert* (London, 1651), p. 192; the allusion helps to date "Upon Appleton House" as posterior to this date. I have supplied the italics.

[57] See in addition to Sabine's work, A. S. P. Woodhouse, *Puritanism and Liberty* (London, 1938); W. Haller, *Rise of Puritanism* (New York, 1938); and T. C. Pease, *The Leveller Movement* (New York, 1916). Whitelocke's *Memorials* and the *Clarke Papers* can also be consulted for this moment of civil excitement.

retirement is not safety. No man is entirely secure, and for a soldier, action may be the fit solution. With his patron advised, Marvell will now talk about himself, and his own bosom-searching occupies the next twenty-two stanzas. It is a poetic chapter from his intellectual and spiritual auto-biography.

Twenty years after he wrote "Upon Appleton House," the poet repeated the sense of these stanzas in the prose of *The Rehearsal Transprosed.*

> Whether it be a war of religion or of liberty it is not worth the labour to inquire. Whichsoever was at the top, the other was at the bottom; but upon considering all, I think the cause was too good to have been fought for. Men ought to have trusted God—they ought to have trusted the King with that whole matter. The arms of the Church are prayers and tears, the arms of the subject are patience and petitions. The King himself being of so accurate and piercing a judgment would soon have felt it where it stuck. *For men may spare their pains when Nature is at work, and the world will not go faster for our driving.*[58]

The prose, written by Milton's colleague and the Member for Hull, expresses a mature conclusion; the stanzas before us pose the propositions and the inner debate. All of this happens in Fairfax's forest, but it is also the woodland of the poet's mind. The Hebraic background that was expressed in the garden and the mowing scenes is now explicit when Marvell-Noah escapes from "the Flood" and takes "Sanctuary" in the "green, yet growing Ark" of the holy wood. We are also in the wilderness where Christ contemplated his mission for forty days, an event foreshadowed when Noah spent the forty days and nights of the Deluge in understanding the ways of God with men. When it is all over, when "the Waves are fal'n and dry'd,/ And now the Meadows fresher

[58] *Works*, ed. Grosart (London, 1872–1875), III, 175.

dy'd," the poet, like the patriarch, will come out of sanctuary
into another world.

To understand this section, we must read "Upon the Hill
and Grove at Bill-Borow," because both forests speak with
us in the same language. They are both "ancient" and, hence,
holy; in both, the union of the houses of Fairfax and Vere
is commemorated. The grove, a preface to the wood, talks
of mutual love and the genius of both houses. They are
also both trees and *a* tree, the heraldic tree of pedigree. Man,
says Marvell, repeating the old image, is an inverted tree,
and so in both poems men are likewise trees. In "Upon
Appleton House" (LXII), we hear about the growing trees
and those that were cut for military use; and we know that
the poet is talking, as the trees are, about the sons of the
illustrious line. "Of whom though many fell in War,/ Yet
more to Heaven shooting are." This is the wood. In the grove,
the trees are also soldiers: "Groves of Pikes he thundered
then." The pikes are both men and trees, and the trees also
provide the military and civil crowns that the house has
merited. The grove, however, gives Marvell a chance for
recording a domestic event in the history of the family.
"*Vera* the Nymph that him inspir'd,/ To whom he often
here retir'd,/ And on these Okes ingrav'd her Name." The
word "retirement" is here, and "Vere" becomes "*Vera*."
But there is more than this in the scene in the grove, for
the passage carries us back to a happy moment in the early
history of Rome.

Instructed by the Camena Egeria, who had married him
and led him into the assemblies of her sisters in the sacred
groves, Numa, second king of the Romans, refined and revised
the religion of the state. He reformed the college of pontiffs;
he instructed the augurs, who knew the will of the gods; he
purified the flamens, who conducted divine worship; he reformed the Vestals and the Salii. He prescribed the rites of

worship and the form of prayer; he even forced Jupiter to
reveal his purposes through thunder and bird flight. He,
then, secured from the gods release from the necessity of
human sacrifice. So Italy, say the chroniclers [59] of his fame,
was filled with a peace like that of the Golden Age until
Numa, ripe with years, fell quietly asleep and the bereft
nymph melted into a fountain of tears. Marvell returns to the
myth again in the second poem: "And as they Natures Cradle
deckt,/ Will in green Age her Hearse expect." True enough,
the grove is not Aricia, "sylva antiqua"—that is the wood at
Nunappleton—and the nymph, visible enough, is not "Egeria"
or "Belief" but "Vera" or "Truth." When Marvell enters the
wood, he will be tutored by both women.

"The double Wood of ancient Stocks" to which the poet
retires is, of course, the security of the house of Fairfax and
Vere, but it is probably more than this. In a sense, by writing
"Upon Appleton House" and other poems that come from
the same years, he has composed his own "silva" or "ὕλη," [60]
titles by which collections of verse had been known in ancient
times. Statius had named his poetic works of a lesser nature
Silvae, and Ben Jonson called his The Forest. But the wood is
also a place of worship and contemplation, synonymous
with the mind and heart of man,[61] and Marvell is hardly in this
wood before he knows he is on holy ground.

> The arching Boughs unite between
> The Columnes of the Temple green;
> And underneath the winged Quires
> Echo about their tuned Fires.

[59] Besides Plutarch's account, see Livy I.18–21; Cicero De Republica
II.13–15; and Dionysius of Halicarnassus II.58–66.

[60] Suetonius De Viris Inlustribus: De grammaticis 25; Quintilian De
Institutione X.3.17; Cicero De Oratore III.26.103; Aulus Gellius Noctes
Atticae Praef. 4–7; Longinus X.1; XIII.4.

[61] The fullest account of the symbolism of the wood can be found in
John Evelyn, A Discourse of Forest Trees (London, 1679), pp. 252–76.

To live in a holy place is to become holy:

> The Oak-Leaves me embroyder all,
> Between which Caterpillars crawl:
> And Ivy, with familiar trails,
> Me licks, and clasps, and curles, and hales.
> Under this *antick Cope* I move
> Like some great *Prelate of the Grove*.

The retired poet, who enters the inner wood to contemplate, ends as a Gomerite, a Druid priest.

The wood at Nunappleton by artistic land-change becomes a *sylva mentis*, not unlike the *hortus mentis* of "The Nymph." [62] It is a place, dark without but "within/ It opens passable and thin." Encamped behind its growing ramparts, the poet, sheltered from those emotions that rise from within as a result of the stimulation of the senses, will, reason being king, contemplate the history of man in terms of the processes of Nature, for "Nature is at work."

> How safe, methinks, and strong, behind
> These Trees have I incamp'd my Mind;
> Where Beauty, aiming at the Heart,
> Bends in some Tree its useless Dart;
> And where the World no certain Shot
> Can make, or me it toucheth not.
> But I on it securely play,
> And gaul its Horsemen all the Day.

Unwed Marvell, safe behind bole and branch, can laugh at Love's archery; and, moving from pathless place to pathless place, he can have sport with the apocalyptic cavalrymen of the World. The passions of love and ambition cooled in the forest, the mind is enabled to reach a conclusion.

We hardly require the Miltonic echoes in stanza LXXVII to perceive that the experiences of "L'Allegro" and "Il

---

[62] On the garden as mind, see Chapter Six.

Penseroso" are being repeated in Nunappleton's forest. The choir is not the "full voiced Choir below" but "the winged Quires" above. In Milton's poem, the voices are human; here it is Nature speaking through the birds. Adam could speak the language of birds; Marvell can only whistle while they listen. But the birds, feathered symbols that they are, instruct the "Churl" by the more eloquent language of their actions. Before they teach him the doctrine of the state, good Aristotelians that they are, they give him domestic instruction. First, he is shown the lovelorn nightingale, then the married doves, then the "thrastles" begetting a family, and, finally, the heron sending its mature offspring into the world. The nightingale answers his questions about the profession of poetry; she sits low, but her singing is harkened to by noble oaks and venerable elders. The *"Stock-doves,"* age-old symbols of wedded bliss, may also instruct the hesitant bachelor.

> Yet always, for some Cause unknown,
> Sad pair unto the Elms they moan.
> O why should such a Couple mourn,
> That in so equal Flames do burn!

All the birds are, I expect, inferior in significance to the "hewel," for whose lectures they merely supply the prolegomenon.

The green woodpecker is of the utmost importance; and in order to understand this, we must once again turn to the *Aeneid*. In the seventh book we find Aeneas' companions, who having raised a mound for Misenus, "aggere composito tumuli," a deed that inspired Marvell's conclusion to the mowing scene, depart by sea for a new land. They skirt the Circean shores, and, looking across the flood, see the great forest filled with birds. "Variae circumque supraque/ Adsuetae ripis volucres." [63] Meanwhile in Latium, King Latinus wor-

[63] 32–33.

ships in the grove near high Albunea and hears the oracle speak from the depth of the wood. Latinus, we remember, is the son of Faunus, who was the son of "Laurentian Picus." Vergil, like Marvell, describes the palace of the King, where he finds the effigy of the augur Picus, holding the regalia of office. According to the Roman, this great King, son of Saturn, was changed by his jealous bride Circe into "picus," the woodpecker. "Fecit avem Circe sparsitque coloribus alas." [64] The myth of the transformation of Picus into picus is told with slight variations by Ovid, Silius Italicus, and many other poets and mythographers, [65] enabling the legend to hallow the bird and make it a quasi-religious symbol.

But the woodpecker is more than a priest, for the Latins associated the bird with the God of War, and usually speak of it as "picus Martius." It is the bird that companions the fiery God as the eagle consorts with Jupiter and the dove with Venus. Picus, however, was a son of Saturn, and so it is not illogical that he is also identified with Jupiter. [66] This makes the "hewel" a symbol of justice as well as of war and religion. I cannot assume that Marvell intends any of these meanings, but when he watches the bird cleaning the Royal Oak of wood moths, when he sees it make its hollow in the tree, rotten because of the "Traitor-worm," he is, I think, learning from nature that the Royal Oak, having fallen by the "*feeble Strok*' " of the bird, is also preserved, because the worms that hollowed it are dead. As Nature restores herself through death, so the state is revivified by the forces of war,

[64] 191.

[65] *Metamorphoses* XIV.390–96; Silius Italicus *Punica* VIII.440–44; Augustine *De Civitate* XVIII.15; Antonius Liberalis *Metamorphoseos* CXIX; *Scriptores Rerum Mythicarum*, ed. Bode (Cellis, 1834), I ,182; II, 213. The account in Boccaccio is interestingly moralized; see *Della Genealogia* (Venice, 1585), p. 140. For its association with Mars, see Plutarch *Quaest. Rom.* XXI; Pliny *Nat. Hist.* X.40.

[66] See Suidas *ad loc.*; and for the Renaissance summary, Aldrovandus, *Ornithologia* (Bologna, 1641), I, 835.

that are also those of religion and justice. The conclusion of
stanza LXX may point to something specific. The oak may
be Charles; the worm may be Strafford or Laud, or someone
else. Howell, the author of *Dodona's Grove*, would probably
know.

Having been tutored by the woodpecker in the natural
processes that bring, without much human intervention, alterations in the affairs of men, Marvell reads further in the "*Sibyls
Leaves*" of "*Natures mystick Book*." In these leaves, which
are now history, he notices the same natural changes affecting
the alterations in the political life of Greece, Rome, and
Palestine. He finds in each history stories of the overthrow of
kings and internal political ferment. He seems to say that in
the natural progression of history, the prelate of the grove
should observe, as he does in the glosses on the Book of Creatures, the writing of the divine hand. He says this by what
seems to me to be an elaborate pun. All of the history of the
past, through which I can make predictions of the future,
says Marvell, "I in this light *Mosaick* read." The word under-
scored by the poet has two possible meanings. First, it may
mean the sunlight that filters through the mosaic of the
leaves overhead; second, and more mystically, it may mean the
Light that Moses, also brooding in the wilderness, saw in the
blazing bush. Marvell is like Moses in the wilderness but he
is also an Aeneas who has gone into the forest, seen the
Sybil, and seen the doves (but not those of Venus). The
Golden Bough has become for him "The Bird upon the
Bough," and Avernus is the memory of the human past. He
must now emerge to read the future, not of the Roman, but
of "the Fairfacian Oak."

When Marvell leaves the wood to sing the future of his
patron's race, he has, I think, solved his own problem to his
immediate satisfaction. He will be the nightingale singing
among the lowly thorns. This is the place he hopes "he may
never leave." He has advised his patron against retirement as

best he can, holding up to him his magisterial duties, the excellence of his qualifications, the urgent necessities of the state of England, and the spiritual impotence and danger of withdrawal from the active life. He knew in his heart of hearts that Fairfax would remain aloof; so he makes his last effort—by praising Mary, he makes a Vergilian comparison. Augustus' line ended with Julia; the fortunes of the House of Fairfax depend on Mary.

The last section of "Upon Appleton House" is in some ways a playful continuation of the founder-myth, the second section of the poem which I have scanted in my analysis. The earlier stanzas (XI–XXXV) are a satire of conventual life and suit the pen of the author of the pamphlets against L'Estrange. The house, built from the nunnery's ruin, was also built when the great ancestor ruined the nuns by carrying off his bride. Fairfax is supposed to read the section as an exhortation to action. Sir William opposed convention and his religious conscience to gain his wife; the current family owes its actual existence to this act. We must now, says Marvell, bring the past to meet the present, "find a *Fairfax* for our *Thwaites.*" The "great *Prelate of the Grove*" comes forward to cut the "*sprig of Misleto.*" So these parts are brought together as history and prophecy, as "scatter'd *Sibyls* Leaves" and the "light Mosaick."

The tradition that controls this final section is not unknown to us; it descends from Vergil through Ariosto, Trissino, and Tasso to Spenser and Marvell. It is the conventional epic vision of the patron's noble line; but Marvell, as is his custom, gives tradition an individual turn. He has been fishing poetically by the stream, just as a fisherman, like Walton, might try for strikes in Aganippe's Well; then he puts aside his hooks, angles, and quills because

> The *young Maria* walks to night:
> Hide trifling Youth thy Pleasures slight.
> 'Twere shame that such judicious Eyes

Should with such Toyes a Man surprize;
She that already is the *Law*
Of all her *Sex,* her *Ages Aw.*

Granting the excesses of seventeenth-century poetical compliment, this (and we can assume that Jonson would agree) is pushing the praise of a twelve-year-old (the precocity of yesterday's children and the affectionate humor of the poet admitted) beyond the fence of decorum. Without question, high compliment is being expended on both Mary and her parents, but just as the "She" of Donne's *Anniversaries* is sometimes Elizabeth and sometimes a *persona symbolica,* so Mary Fairfax is possibly sometimes herself and sometimes another person. The facts are undoubtedly accurate. The girl was "Pure, Sweet, Streight, and Fair"; she showed a talent for languages; she was about to be sought in marriage by many young aristocrats; she had been born into "a Domestic Heaven" and knew the lures of foolish vanity; and, a male heir wanting, she would get the Fairfax *"Goodness"* in entail. She is, however, more than this, and Marvell, as is his custom, supplies the key to her mystery.

One of the hints about Mary's true nature is granted by Milton, whose "Ode on the Morning of Christ's Nativity" stands behind this section of "Upon Appleton House" in the way that "L'Allegro" and "Il Penseroso" stand behind the woodland stanzas. One should first notice that in both poems the appearance of a special person in the realm of Nature results in a calm and quiet that is almost static. In Marvell's poem, Nature puts forth "its *Bonne Mine";* in Milton's she "doffs her gaudy trim." In Milton it is the "Winds with wonder whist"; in Marvell "every thing" is "whisht and fine." In both poems the sun's bedroom is described; though Marvell's sun, unlike Milton's, is a modest bachelor. The halcyon flies in both poems to insure calm. In the "Nativity Ode" the oracles "are dum"; in "Upon Appleton House" *"Admiring*

Nature" is benumbed by "an horror calm and dumb." In the poem of 1629, the shepherds are taken by a "blissful rapture" comparable to Marvell's: "And men the silent *Scene* assist,/ Charm'd with the *Saphir-winged Mist.*" And there is possibly a memory of Milton's "The Stars with deep amaze/ Stand fixt in steadfast gaze,/ Bending one way their precious influence" in Marvell's "No new-born *Comet* such a Train/ Draws through the Skie, nor Star new-slain." In both poems, we are in the presence of wonder. To understand the identity of Marvell's wonder we must return to "*She* that already is the *Law.*"

The appearance of Mary in the twilight hour produces tranquillity. She is accompanied, almost as if she were a goddess, by the halcyon; in fact, it is almost as if she had become the mythical Alcyone herself. The bird, famous as a symbol of peace and calm, appears, as Vergil informs us, in the hush between the setting of the sun and the first rays of the evening star.

> Tum tenuis dare rursus aquas et pascere rursus
> Solis ad occasum, cum frigidus aera vesper
> Temperat, et saltus reficit iam roscida luna
> Litoraque alcyonem resonant. . . .[67]

The Greek pastoral poets, Theocritus [68] and Moschus,[69] had praised the miracle of this bird; and Lucian's Socrates, describing the peace that it brings, asks his friend to observe the halcyon's world "calm and serene even in mid-winter; see how clear the sky, the whole ocean at peace, smooth as a looking-glass." [70] The fact that Mary is given this bird as a heraldic device suggests that she is to be associated with tranquillity and peace, but she is also linked in stanzas LXXXVII–

---

[67] *Georgics* III.335–38.
[68] VII.57–59.
[69] III.40–41.
[70] *Halcyon* 2.

LXXXVIII with the perfection of those early poetical topics: gardens, woods, meadows, and streams. In stanza LXXX, she has something to do with wisdom of a heavenly kind: "Nor yet that *Wisdome* would affect,/ But as 'tis *Heavens Dialect*." She is also a war maiden, who stands off the attacks and foils the amorous ambushes of soldier-lovers. We are told that she excels all other women in virtue and knowledge, and that she is the virgin of virgins: "That, as all *Virgins* She preceds." We have left the halcyon for this account of the girl who also brings peace, adds grace to the things of nature, is war-like, and gifted with heavenly wisdom. The bird returns now to tell us in the words of Antipater of Sidon that its mistress is the goddess Pallas Athena: "ἱστῶν Παλλάδος ἀλκυόνα." [71]

It is possibly this goddess, so important in the statecraft of Athens and Rome, whom Marvell hides behind the figure of Mary Fairfax. She was the virgin of virgins, as superior to all goddesses in chastity as she was their superior in wisdom. We hardly need go beyond the *Iliad* and the *Odyssey* to establish her central virtues. She maintained law and order in the state.[72] She can fight against external enemies, but she is not a female counterpart of Ares;[73] for she restrains men from slaughter, reproving and even defeating the great God of War.[74] She has no weapons of her own, but must borrow her armor from Zeus.[75] Through her, men learned the arts of agriculture, for she invented the tools of the field and created the peaceful olive. For these reasons Vergil invokes her as a patroness of his *Georgics:* "Adsis . . . oleaeque Minerva inventrix." [76] It is Athena, or Minerva, who adds her qualities to gardens, woods, meadows and stream, the topics of Marvell's song.

[71] *Anthol. Pal.* VI.160.
[72] *Odyssey* XIII.394ff.
[73] *Iliad* V.736.
[74] *Ibid.,* V.840; XXI.406.
[75] *Ibid.,* I.199.
[76] I.18–19.

It is, however, her heavenly wisdom that accounted for all her other powers. Homer gives her the epithet of "many-counseled," "πολύβουλος Ἀθήνη," [77] the same epithet that he applies to her father, Zeus. But it is the poet Plato to whom we can turn for a full understanding of her powers. Let us listen to a lecture in philology delivered by Socrates to Hermogenes.

That is a weightier matter, my friend, and here the modern explainers of Homer help us to understand the ancient belief about Athene. Most of these in commenting on the poet say that by Athene he meant *mind* (νοῦς) and *intellect* (διάνοια); and the maker of her name seems to have had the same notion about her but he gives her the still grander title of "the mind of God" (ἡ θεοῦ νόησις), as if he would say: "This is she who has the mind of God" (ἁ θεονόα), using here the alpha in a foreign way for eta and eliding the iota and sigma. Perhaps, however, this was not his reason; he may have called her Theonoë to mean "she who knows divine matters" (τὰ θεῖα νοοῦσα). He may, perhaps, have wished to identify her with moral wisdom (ἐν ἤθει νόησις) by calling her Ethonoë, which he, or his successors thought they improved when they called her Athenaa.[78]

The nature of the mistress of the halcyon as "the mind of God" or as "divine wisdom" is here made plain. The Greek position is, of course, not enough, and we may remember the Christian equivalent. The goddess Athena was able to cross frontiers; in the Christian world, she was known as Sophia and there was a poem about her.

In the *Sophia Salomonos* the heroine, like her Greek prototype, is an emanation rather than a creation of God. She is arrayed in a series of epithets; she is finer than a lily of the fields. She is "the vapor of the power of God," "a pure emanation of the glory," "reflection of eternal light," "a spotless mir-

---

[77] *Iliad* V.260; see also Hesiod *Theogony* 886–900, and the Homeric "Hymn to Athena."
[78] *Cratylus* 407A–C.

ror." [79] When the poet adds that she lives in closeness with God [80] and is his grand manifestation,[81] he repeats, probably without knowing it, the sort of praise that the pagans rendered to Athena. But Sophia is more than Athena, more than that great golden figure laden with ivory; for she existed, we are told, before the Creation,[82] and assisted in the making of the universe.[83] Since then she has not rested because she is the artificer of all things.[84] Solomon's poem is mainly addressed to kings who would rule righteously and with justice, but it can also be read by all men who follow the divine light, men like Marvell who read in *"Natures mystick Book."* "For she knows the things of old and conjectures the things to come." [85]

The second half of the *Sophia Salomonos* proclaims the "great She" as the inspirer of the kings and captains of Israel. Here Solomon, like his English disciple, makes the story of the Exodus his chief example of Sophia's gifts. She led the chosen of God through the deep sea, and "cast them up out of the depths of the abyss"; [86] she provided quail food and manna for the starving. She is also a composer of apocalyptic paradoxes, who takes us back to stanza LX.

> For land creatures were turned into water creatures,
> And swimming creatures migrated on earth.
> Fire had control of its own power in water,
> And water forgot its own power of extinguishing,
> Flames wasted not the flesh of perishable creatures
> That walked among them, nor was melted
> The easily melted ice-like heavenly food.[87]

[79] 7:25–26.
[80] 8:3–4.
[81] 9:9.
[82] 9:1.
[83] 6:14; 9:4.
[84] 7:22.
[85] 8:8.
[86] 10:18–19.
[87] 19:19–21.

Behind the child Mary and her human virtues stands the pagan wisdom of Athena and of Sophia, the graver and more potent daughter of Jehovah.

If there is a solemn conclusion to the poem it is that divine wisdom must come in this moment of half-light to guide the land of Britain, the erstwhile general, and the poet who celebrates both state and man. Through her, Marvell implies, and through her alone will the garden and the wood be restored. Even the world, which was originally created as a smooth sphere, and is now because of the Flood "All negligently overthrown," still is preserved by divine wisdom. As Marvell writes this, darkness comes like a black bowl over the world; it almost seems as if Atlas had come up from the mere with a leather boat hoisted over his head or as if Alastor, the black one, had entered the temple during the gods' absence. This darkness is also known to Sophia. It is that of lawless men, who think to hold a nation in their power: by "one chain of darkness" all are bound so that even if birds sing, and water falls, and hills echo, and all of Nature is bathed in light, "Over them alone heavy night was spread,/ An image of darkness which was to receive them;/ But to themselves they were heavier than darkness." [88] Sophia may be represented in Mary, but Mary is a charming little girl and not Sophia. "Let's in," says the teasing Marvell, "for the dark *Hemisphere,*/ Does now like one of them appear." This is an amusing conclusion and it is typically Vergilian, but it also goes as far beyond Vergil as Divine Wisdom surpasses Athena. In spite of the speculation in the garden and in the wood, dark without but light within, the black clouds hang over the island's fortunes. "Let's in," says the poet, let us come out of the night and seek the light in the house. " 'Twas no Religious House till now."

[88] 17: 15–20.

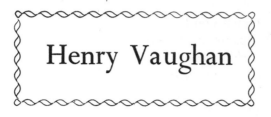

CHAPTER EIGHT

Henry Vaughan

"Cock-Crowing"

Vaughan lived in the narrow space between two worlds: one was a world of crystal translucency and one was of blind darkness. The black world he knew sadly enough and well; the world of light he saw indistinctly because the veil of mortality thwarted his vision: "And onely see through a long night/ Thy edges and thy bordering light." [1] The veil, which Christ alone had penetrated [2] and which Vaughan knew would cover his eyes until Doomsday, [3] becomes a constant symbol of the poet's spiritual frustration. He lives "under veyls here"; [4] he hopes to have "his Curtaines off"; [5] or he awaits the time when his "callous veyl" [6] will be purged away by fire. His realization

[1] *Works*, ed. L. C. Martin (Oxford, 1914), p. 521.
[2] P. 485.
[3] P. 542.
[4] P. 535.
[5] P. 399.
[6] P. 396.

of spiritual insufficiency has, on occasion, a conscious edge of violence:

> Since in these veyls my Ecclips'd Eye
> May not approach thee, (for at night
> Who can have commerce with the light?)
> I'le disapparell, and to buy
> But one half glaunce, most gladly dye.[7]

It is not enough for him that at times he sees the great Light in dreams or in visions that are almost ecstatic; but, fortunately, the failure of spiritual sight is not a prompter of mortal despair. Vaughan remembers his "glimpses" and he is cheered by the knowledge that a candle shines on "some heads,"[8] that in him is the seed, the tiny inner warmth, "That Sacred Ray/ Thy Spirit plant."[9] Sometimes his deeds mist within him "and put out that lamp";[10] sometimes this ray, a star captive in a tomb, cannot blaze with the full ardor of the stars;[11] yet he is blessed when he finds that all creatures, even those lesser than he, possess a glimmering of the secret light.

All creatures, he tells us in "Palm Sunday," have an interior flickering that permits them to recognize their incarnate Creator.[12] Vaughan wishes to share in this gift, to interpret with the birds the splendid doctrine of Providence.[13] He yearns to be a star or a bird; then he "should be/ Shining, or singing still to Thee."[14] The doctrine of the world of light is partially expressed in "The Eagle,"[15] but from time to time he recalls

[7] P. 419.
[8] P. 395.
[9] P. 448.
[10] P. 433.
[11] P. 421.
[12] P. 501.
[13] P. 506.
[14] P. 422.
[15] P. 606.

the old contention between light and darkness and knows that
he is on the edge of a terrible forest.

> But as these Birds of light make a land glad,
> Chirping their solemn Matins on each tree:
> So in the shades of night some dark fowls be,
> Whose heavy notes make all that hear them, sad.[16]

The rent between the two worlds is here made plain, but
Vaughan, while doubtful of satisfaction in the veiled life, seeks
constantly to see light in darkness, even though this light is
filtered and is not God's "Center and mid-day." In "Cock-
Crowing" he selects the bird of light as a commanding symbol. Here he can gloss darkness by light and know his own
soul in terms of a lesser creature. Before we trace the history
of this symbol, we should read the poem.

> Father of lights! what Sunnie seed,
> What glance of day hast thou confin'd
> Into this bird? To all the breed
> This busie Ray thou hast assign'd;
> Their magnetisme works all night,
> And dreams of Paradise and light.

> Their eyes watch for the morning hue,
> Their little grain expelling night
> So shines and sings, as if it knew
> The path unto the house of light.
> It seems their candle, howe'r done,
> Was tinn'd and lighted at the sunne.

> If such a tincture, such a touch,
> So firm a longing can impowre
> Shall thy own image think it much
> To watch for thy appearing hour?
> If a meer blast so fill the sail,
> Shall not the breath of God prevail?

[16] P. 497.

O thou immortall light and heat!
Whose hand so shines through all this frame,
That by the beauty of the seat,
We plainly see, who made the same.
Seeing thy seed abides in me,
Dwell thou in it, and I in thee.

To sleep without thee, is to die;
Yea, 'tis a death partakes of hell:
For where thou dost not close the eye
It never opens, I can tell.
In such a dark, Ægyptian border,
The shades of death dwell and disorder.

If joyes, and hopes, and earnest throws,
And hearts, whose Pulse beats still for light
Are given to birds; who, but thee, knows
A love-sick souls exalted flight?
Can souls be track'd by any eye
But his, who gave them wings to flie?

Onely this Veyle which thou hast broke,
And must be broken yet in me,
This veyle, I say, is all the cloke
And cloud which shadows thee from me.
This veyle thy full-ey'd love denies,
And onely gleams and fractions spies.

O take it off! make no delay,
But brush me with thy light, that I
May shine unto a perfect day,
And warme me at thy glorious Eye!
O take it off! or till it flee,
Though with no Lilie, stay with me!

This poem is plainly a minor metaphor in the three larger images that are the major centers of Vaughan's poetic theology. There is, first, the seed planted by God in the flinty soil of the human heart, watered by the showers and streams of his

Grace and warmed to growth by the essential light. As the
seed grows, it is whipped by the winds of the world, strangled
by weeds, blighted by the frost of sin. In time it will be a lily,
blossoming to its maker's hand. The growth of the plant from
its green root is likened in a second sense to a great journey
back to the noble, yet "shady City of Palme trees." The trav-
eler often goes, like Nicodemus, by night to find his Lord; and
the way lies through a blasted land, over treacherous rocks
and past dangerous woods. The voyage is sometimes star-
lighted, but often light is shut out by cloud and darkness.
Finally, there is the metaphor of union, when God receives the
flower, and the saved poet returns to the soul-land from
whence he came. "Cock-Crowing" does not overlook any of
these capital topics, but it belongs to the first metaphoric
center, fixing our attention on the seed of light that God, according to Vaughan, has planted in all his creatures. Here the
creature celebrated is the cock, and behind Vaughan's choice
of this bird to expound his doctrine lies the usual tradition,
both pagan and Christian.

In the history of symbols, the mysteries of the cosmos are
frequently suggested by birds that live between heaven and
earth, for wings are necessary to the exploration of celestial
pastures and man must listen to birdsong, as Marvell did, in
order to learn something about celestial harmony. The gods
of the ancients, when not winged themselves, were attended
by significant birds of their own choosing. The eagle accom-
panies Jove as the hawk had once journeyed with Horus; the
peacock is holy to Juno; the dove, to Venus. Though Hades
is a land where no birds sing, the Elysian Fields could not have
been endured or enjoyed without them. Tibullus imagines the
great goddess walking with lovers in the Hereafter and listening to the viols and flutes of choral birds.

> Sed me, quod facilis tenero sum semper Amori,
>   Ipsa Venus compos ducet in Elysios.

> Hic choreae cantusque vigent, passimque vagantes
> Dulce sonant tenui gutture carmen aves.[17]

The cock, master of the raucous song praised in Vaughan's poem, was to antiquity the most familiar of birds, the *dux et rex* of the yard and doorway; yet, though he was common, he was also a holy bird, sacred to Athena, to Hermes, to Latona, to Demeter, and to the half-gods, Hercules and Aesculapius. It was natural that he was the symbol of the sun; and it was for this reason that Idomeneus, the fighting flame of the *Iliad,* who was descended from Helios, bore an effigy of the bird on his shield.[18] For the Greek and Latin world, the rooster was the "bird of light," and as such he not only expelled the dark but the evils that walked by night.

> Nocte Deae Nocti cristatus caeditur ales,
> Quod tepidum vigili provocat ore diem.[19]

The sunless hours, as these lines from Ovid imply, are filled with uncertain dread that the cock with his "instinct of light" (so Heliodorus [20] calls it) banishes. The dread that the pagans define with uncertainty is made clear for us when Basil states that the call of the sun-bird puts demons to flight.[21] The fact that the early Church used the rooster as a funereal ornament and that the bird is mentioned in epitaphic verse is, consequently, not surprising; he is not only the bird of light, but a symbol of the eternal light that guides and protects the souls of the dead. The cock's conversion to Christianity was easy,

[17] I.3.57–60.

[18] Pausanias *Itinerary* V.25.9.

[19] Ovid *Fasti* I.455–56; see *Met.* XI.597–98 and Lucretius *De. Rer. Nat.* IV.710–14.

[20] *Aethiopicus* I.18.3.

[21] J.-F. Boissonade, *Anecdota Graeca* (Paris, 1829–1833), III, 445. The traditional fear of the lion for the cock is recorded by Pliny (X.48), and this account, repeated in the Middle Ages and Renaissance, is read on the basis of Ps. 21:22 and I Pet. 5:8 as an allegory in which the lion is Satan.

and it was facilitated not only by his pagan repute but also by the special qualities that Christian writers gave to all birds.[22]

When Vaughan wrote the first two stanzas of this poem, he was rephrasing in Christian terms what any classical poet might have said. The same classical knowledge helps us read stanzas five, seven, and eight, but we must go to the Scriptures and the tradition of the Church for full comprehension. The cock of St. Peter's denial is supported by an impressive passage in Job (38:36) where the admonishing Jehovah states: "Who placed wisdom in the heart of man, or who gave understanding to the cock?" With this text, men and the bird of dawn are brought together in the benefits of God though their shares are qualitatively different. It is the memory of this fecundating verse and the history of the human symbolism of the cock in

---

[22] Classical poets sometimes gave birds human characteristics. Propertius makes the cock an author: "Tum queror, in toto non sidere pallia lecto,/ Lucis et auctores non dare carmen aves" (IV.3.31–32), and Ovid makes the crow "auctor aquae" (*Amores* II.6.34). Late Latin and mediaeval poets often turn birds into musical instruments or human musicians. Sedulius makes them little organs: "Tempora veris celebrant crespante sussurro,/ Produnt organulis tempora veris aves" (*Poetae Latini Aevi Carolini*, ed. Traube [Berlin, 1896], III, 227). John of Garland has them playing cithers while the organ plays a requiem (G. Mari, "Poetris magistri Johannis Anglici de arte prosayca metrica et rithmica," *Rom. Forsch.*, XIII [1902], 894). St. Jerome in a prose account of spring describes them as singing psalms (*Epistulae*, ed. Hilberg [Vienna, 1910], XLIII, 3). In the *Carmina Burana*, there is a poem describing the nightingale as a cither-player: "Citharizat cantico dulcis philomena" (eds. Hilka and Schumann [Heidelberg, 1951], poem 138, st. 4, l. 1); elsewhere in the same collection, birds are said to sing to the drum, the psalter, the lyre, and the viol (92.60–64), or "melodia sonant garrule" (151.2). Alanus de Insulis relates them to sirens and gives them many musical duties: "Syrenes nemorum, cytharistae veris,/ in illum/ Convenere locum, mellitaque carmina sparsim/ Commentantur aves, dum gutturis organa pulsant./ Pingunt ore lyram, dum cantus imbibit istos/ Auditus, dulces effert sonus auribus escas" (*Anticlaudianus, The Minor Anglo-Latin Satirists*, ed. Wright [London, 1872], II, 276). The idea that birds are poets as well as authors is suggested in early Italian literature: "E gli augelletti riprendon lor lena/ E fanno dolci versi in loro usanza" (*Early Italian Literature*, ed. Grillo [London, 1920], I, 213).

the Christian world that effect the transition between the first and last stanzas of Vaughan's poem. The Christian cock is the Christian man; so a poem is produced that is, in all it says, an invocation. What comes from God is thus returned to him.

To bring this about, the pagan symbolism of the cock combines with Biblical expressions to make the Christian symbol. It is St. Ambrose who provided poets with the text on the cock that filled their imaginations with crowing metaphors.

> When this bird sings, the highwayman leaves his ambush, for the morning star, called forth, rises and lights the heaven. With this singing, the anxious sailor puts aside sorrow, for the tempests and storms stirred up by the strong night winds are quieted. The devout man, moved by this singing, rises to pray and to read the offices. Finally, with this song, the cornerstone of the Church himself washes away his sin contracted by denying when once before the cock crowed. With this song hope returns to all. The tedium of sickness is lightened; the pain of wounds lessens; the heat of fevers lowers; faith returns to the fallen; Jesus regards the hesitant and corrects the wanderers.[23]

With these praises, the cock becomes a Christian bird, for the references in both Testaments have made him the angel at the door, or, as Cassiodorus calls him, "spiritualis gallus." [24] But he is more commonly recognized in the beginning as one of those minor saints, "qui in nocte saeculi per fidem clamant in Dominum," [25] and this is a figuration that would have pleased Vaughan. Once Gregory had written his *Moralia in Job*, the cock became the personal analogue of the priest,[26] a

---

[23] *Hexameron* (PL, XIV, 255).

[24] *Expositio in Psalterium* (PL, CXX, 817).

[25] Pseudo-Jerome, *Expositio* (PL, XXIII, 1529).

[26] PL, LXXVI, 527–28. This account is followed with expansions by Hugo of St. Victor in *De Bestis Aliis et Rebus* (PL, CLXXVII, 33–35); see also St. Eucherius, *Formulae Spiritalis* (PL, L, 750); Rupertus, *Commentarius in*

man divinely moved, who has a special understanding of God's ways and whose duty, like that of the cock, is not only to bring light to men but to warn those who sleep in darkness of the imminent coming of God. The responsibilities of these instructed men on the eve of Doomsday are described by Rupertus with the metaphor of the cock: "And just as the rooster by crowing shakes off with his notes the sleep of sloth, announcing the coming light, the priest . . . ." In Vaughan's final four stanzas, the Christian cock becomes, as tradition will have it, the sign of the Last Judgment.

All of these texts are nonpoetical, and we must turn to the Latin poetry of the Middle Ages to find the literary way to Vaughan. In his great hymn, "Aeterne rerum conditor," Ambrose brought the cock into the liturgy.

> Surgemus ergo strenue,
>   Gallus jactantes excitat,
> Et somnolentes increpat,
>   Gallus negantes arguit.
> Gallo canente, spes redit,
>   Ægris salus refunditur,
> Mucro latronis conditur
>   Lapsis fides revertitur.[27]

Prudentius, the successor of Ambrose, made the bird's place sure when he put him at the entrance of the *Liber Cathemerinon;* here in the "Hymnus ad Galli Cantum," the singing cock awakens men from spiritual slumber, warning them of the coming splendour. "Nostri figura est iudicis," says the poet and then solemnly expands the idea.

> Hic somnus ad tempus datus
>   Est forma mortis perpetis:

Job (PL, CLXVIII, 1163); and *Le Bestiare,* ed. Walberg (Paris, 1900), ll. 230–313.
    [27] *PL,* XVI, 1473.

Peccata, ceu nox horrida,
    Cogunt iacere ac stertere.

Sed vox ab alto culmine
    Christi docentis praemonet
Adesse iam lucem prope,
    Ne mens sopori serviat.

Ne somnus usque ad terminos
    Vitae socordis opprimat
Pectus sepultum crimine
    Et lucis oblitum suae.

Vaughan almost says this in English: "To sleep without thee, is to die;/ Yea, 'tis a death partakes of hell." [28] Prudentius, who strives for the fullest interpretation, continues, reminding his readers that Peter's denial came as Christ conquered Hell and Death. His bird, too, has further lessons for those who sleep in darkness and dream vainly of gold, glory, and pleasure. "Fit mane, nil sunt omnia." For the cock, we are then assured, is not only the herald of God's light, the resonant shout of Doomsday, but also the grave Judge.

Tu, Christe, somnium dissice,
    Tu rumpe noctis vincula,
Tu solve peccatum vetus
    Novumque lumen ingere.[29]

The hymns of Ambrose and Prudentius made the cock a divine analogue, and thereafter he finds a sure place in the ritual. The Mozarabic hymns included one song for matins, "Gallo canente venimus" [30] and in two other hymns—"Gallus

---

[28] Vaughan's "dark Ægyptian border," which also appears in "The Relapse" as "a thick, Egyptian damp" (p. 433) has a symbolism of sin and sinners; see Tertullian, *De Spectaculis* (*PL*, I, 635); and St. Prosper, *Psalmorum . . . Expositio* (*PL*, LI, 326).

[29] *Carmina*, ed. Dressel (Leipzig, 1860), pp. 4–9.

[30] *PL*, LXXXVI, 935.

diei nuntius"[31] and "Gallus auroram resonis/ Salutans canti-
bus"[32]—the bird has a symbolic rôle. The poets of the age of
Charlemagne naturally celebrated the priestly rooster who
called men to worship[33] and who predicted the day of God's
Coming.[34] The latter theme is handsomely embroidered in
the *Carmina Centulensis*, where the poet presents the cock
and the thrush singing a doomsong together after the morning
choir; a relatively somber hymn it is, in which they urge the
righteous to prepare immediately for the new age of gold.[35] But
all of these poems are minor compared to the fourteenth-
century, "Multi sunt presbyteri qui ignorant, quare/ Super
domum domini gallus solet stare."

By the time this poem was written the cock had obviously
taken a firm perch on spires, and this poem attempts to tell us
why he is so honored. Throughout this poem, the mutual
duties of priest and layman are carefully annotated in terms of
the symbolic legend of the cock; for though the cock is a
priest in analogy—"si bonus presbyter eius fit figura"—the
secular can also take instruction from the bird. Actually, the
poem is a series of contrasts. The care of the bird for his flock
is balanced against the fact that the hellish basilisk is hatched
from his eggs. "Sic crescit diabolus ex presbyterorum/ Magna
negligentia." Once more we hear of the cock as a mighty
ward against evil, of his strict warnings in God's service, of
his premonitions of the Day of Judgment.

> Sic et bonus presbyter, respuens terrena,
> Ducat suos subditos ex inferni poena,

[31] J.-F. Gergier, *Lyricus Sacer* (Bensaçon, 1889), R, poem 21.
[32] J. Santolius, *Hymni Sacri et Novi* (Paris, 1698), p. 192.
[33] Paulus Albarus, *Carmina*, ed. Traube, *PLAC* (Berlin, 1896), III, 128.
[34] Milo, *Carmina*, *PLAC*, III, 582–84, 661.
[35] III.332. There is an enigma on the cock by Tatwin (Wright, II, 543)
in which the bird is associated with adventual prophecies.

> Praebens iter caelicum caeli per amoena
> Ut cum Christus venerit, turba sit serena.[36]

Without this tradition, Vaughan's poem might not have
come into being in the text that we have; with the tradition,
it is richer and fuller in all its implications. For centuries before Vaughan saw visions by the Usk, the cock had been
famed for his instinctive knowledge of light, not only that of
the lesser light of the sun but also of the divine light. For this
reason he was associated with the priest as an expeller of spiritual darkness and of evil. In the natural world he made lions
afraid; in the higher world, he was victor over the lions of
Hell. While he reminded men of their duties to God and
roused them from their worldly slumber, he also warned them
of Christ's Second Coming and urged them to prepare for the
Day of Judgment. These traditions make the fabric of the
early and late stanzas of "Cock-Crowing," but there is another
connection that must be established because Vaughan says
that the bird has within him a "busie Ray," "a little grain ex-
pelling night," whereas man, "thy own image," has a soul that
is far broader in its comprehension of the divine. Hence, if
the rooster can dream "of Paradise and light,"

> Shall thy own image think it much
> To watch for thy appearing hour?

The difference between man and the cock implies the difference between "sapientia" and "intelligentia." For Vaughan
this difference is expressed by the breeze that fills a sail and
that which fills the soul of the poet, the very breath of God.
But as the poem proceeds, the soul becomes like a bird.

> If joyes, and hopes, and earnest throws
> And hearts, whose Pulse beats still for light

[36] *The Oxford Book of Medieval Latin Verse*, ed. Gaslee (Oxford, 1925),
pp. 178-80.

> Are given to birds; who, but thee, knows
> A love-sick souls exalted flight?
> Can souls be track'd by any eye
> But his, who gave them wings to flie?

The translation of soul into bird is also part of a long poetic process.

Drawing on the bank of pagan symbolism, the early Christians associated the soul with flying things. The Greeks had represented the soul as a winged replica of the person who was dead, and Psyche, the soul-butterfly, set the pattern for the iconographical description of the Christian soul with her colored wings.[37] The relationship between the soul or mind of man, and birds, was strongly perceived by the Greeks, and it is not surprising to find that Plato compares the mind to an aviary,[38] or that Plotinus discovers three kinds of souls among men and compares them to three classes of birds.[39] This decorous symbol was appropriated by the Fathers of Christian belief because it was also authorized by the Scriptures.

As we stand at the deathbeds of the saints of antiquity, we see, if we believe their chroniclers, their souls ascending to heaven as birds. St. Benedict saw the soul of his sister, leaving her body in the form of a dove; [40] and St. Gregory in his record of the death of Abbot Spes says that the soul of that devout man was seen "in columbae specie." [41] In the *Peristephanon*, Prudentius turns his experience into poetry.

> Emicat inde columba repens
> Martyris os nive candidior
> Visa relinquere et astra sequi;
> Spiritus hic erat Eulaliae
> Lacteolus, celer, innocuus.

[37] See Chapter Two.
[38] *Theaetetus* 197C.
[39] *Enneads* V.9.1, 6–21.
[40] *Prolegomena* (PL, LXVI, 196).
[41] *Dialogi* (PL, LXXVII, 336).

Colla fluunt abeunte anima
Et rogus igneus emoritur,
Pax datur artubus exanimis,
Flatus in aethere plaudit ovans
Templaque celsa petit volucer.

Vidit et ipse satelles avem
Feminae ab ore meare palam,
Obstupefactus et attonitus
Prosilit et sua gesta fugit,
Lictor et ipse fugit pavidus.[42]

Though for most early Christian poets the soul assumes the form of a dove or a nameless bird,[43] the Renaissance was also able to associate the soul with the cock. The translation is due not to Christian tradition, but once again, to Plato.

"I owe, Crito," says the dying Socrates, "a cock to Aesculapius; do not forget to pay it." The interpretation of this final request of the great philosopher has caused men of all times to whip their minds. The irreverent Lucian observes that the remark shows what little regard Socrates had for Zeus.[44] The testimony of this scoffer was hardly acceptable to early Christians; yet, in this case, Tertullian agrees with the pagan and observes that Socrates, the atheist, ordered the sacrifice out of filial consideration for his father.[45] Origen thinks the demand shows that Socrates, in spite of his wisdom, abandoned eminent principles for the trivial and unimportant.[46] Chrysostom [47] and Theodoret [48] smell idolatry. Lactantius is more brutal: Socrates feared the judge of the dead, stern Rhadamanthus.[49]

[42] *Op. cit.*, p. 338.
[43] See Rabanus Maurus (*PL*, CXII, 871); Rupertus (*PL*, CLXVIII, 294); Garnerus de St. Victor (*PL*, CXCIII, 65).
[44] *Bis. Accus.* 5.
[45] *Ad Nationes* (*PL*, I, 589).
[46] *Contra Celsum* (*PG*, XI, 1294).
[47] *Commentarius in Epistolam ad Romanos* (*PG*, LX, 414).
[48] *Graecorum Affectionum Curatio* (*PG*, LXXXIII, 1006).
[49] *Institutiones Divinae* (*PL*, VI, 417).

The humanists, to whom Plato was the master that Aristotle
was to the scholastics, rose to the defence of their philosopher.
Ficino saw in the dying request of Socrates a statement of
Christian intent. Socrates, he insists, sought among the gods for
a physician who could cure the diseases of the soul; and when
at last he had resolved his own diseases (doubts and fears), he
was eager to thank God.[50] Pico della Mirandola fully agrees
with his friend and extends the allegory. The cock, he states,
is the soul of man; this is the reason that Socrates said he owed
a cock to Aesculapius. By this ultimate statement he meant
that he owed his own soul to the great doctor of souls.[51] So
for the Florentine Platonists the cock of the *Phaedo* was the
soul of the philosopher, but their concept was strengthened by
another citation in the books of the past.

As every educated man of the seventeenth century knew,
there is among the cryptic and almost mystical sayings of
Pythagoras the strict advice: "Feed the cock." The baffling
command was explained by the sixteenth-century editor,
Lilius Gyraldus—a great explainer of enigmas—as golden doctrine. Pythagoras, he tells us, was encouraging his disciples to
feed the divine part of the soul (the cock) with celestial
knowledge just as they fed their bodies with more mundane
food.[52] So the cock of Erasmus' St. Socrates and the cock of
Milton's St. Pythagoras become in the sixteenth century the
immortal soul of man. The symbol of solar light arrives with
pagan help at a greater definition, for it changes into the
"seed," the created light that dwells in all humankind.

With this alteration we can better understand how Vaughan
could move from the allegory of the cock to the Christian
desires of his inner self. Behind much of the transformation

[50] Plato, *Opera* (Lyons, 1548), p. 333.
[51] *Commentationes* (Bologna, 1496), p. 134r.
[52] *Pythagorae Symbolorum Interpretatio*, in *Opera* (Leyden, 1696), II,
659–60.

may rest his philosophical belief in the mysterious doctrines of the universe that he shared with his brother,[53] but enforcing these and making them real is the poetical result of the long struggle of men to express in terms of the lower world what their hearts tell them about the unknowable. In the darkness, the heart of flint sparks, and from its little lights the poet gains courage to await the rending of the veil. The seed has grown into a plant though the plant may not yet have brought forth a bright flower.

> O take it off! make no delay,
> But brush me with thy light, that I
> May shine unto a perfect day,
> And warme me at thy glorious Eye!
> O take it off! or till it flee,
> Though with no Lilie, stay with me!

In this last stanza, reminded by the cock, Vaughan writes his own "Venite rerum Conditor"; but as he writes it, he also realizes that the time may be far away, that he may have to visit with the night before he sees the eternal brightness of God. He draws his comfort and he frames his prayer according to the text of the creature instinct with light. This symbol remains with us, for Vaughan's cock crows again for Masefield.

> But in the darkest hour of night
> When even the foxes peer for light
> The byre-cock crows; he feels the light.
>
> So, in this water mixed with dust
> The byre-cock spirit crows from trust
> That death will change because it must.

---

[53] See *The Works of Thomas Vaughan*, ed. Waite (London, 1919), pp. 81–82, 266–67.

Index of Authors and Editors

Achilles Tatius, 127
Adam of St. Victor, 77
Aeschylus, 132
Alanus ab Insulis, 40, 112, 160
Albarus, Paulus, 164
Alciati, A., 12, 134
Aldhelm, 77
Aldrovandus, U., 137, 145
Alexis, Guillaume, 10
Alleaume, M., 124
Ambrose, Saint, 74-5, 77, 88, 109, 161-3
Anacreon, 70-1, 82-3, 88
Anglicus, J., 160
Antipater of Sidon, 150
Antonius Liberalis, 96, 145
Apollodorus, 97
Apollonius of Rhodes, 45, 131
Apuleius, 26-8, 30
Arber, E., 13
Ariosto, L., 34, 53, 71, 147
Aristophanes, 61
Aristotle, 168
Arnobius, 96
Athenaeus, 109
Auber, C. A., 38
Augustine, Saint, 28, 109, 145
Aulus Gellius, 142
Ausonius, 9, 68, 72, 76, 113
Avitus, Saint, 75

Baif, A., 6, 16, 71-2
Baldi, B., 64
Barbazan, E., 71
Barrois, J. B., 99
Basel, Saint, 159
Bastin, J., 88
Bede, Saint, 101
Belleau, 12, 71, 82
Bello, F., 53
Bembo, P., 106
Benedict, Saint, 166
Benevenuto de Imola, 31
Berneville, G. de, 101
Berni, F., 124
Beroaldus, P., 28, 30
Bessarion, 28
Beza, T., 54
Bion, 1-2, 4-6, 8-9, 11, 19, 78
Blake, H., 28
Blanchemain, P., 13, 105, 110
Boccaccio, G., 28-9, 145
Bode, G. H., 145
Boer, C. de, 39
Boileau, N., 22
Boissonade, J.-F., 159
Bos, A., 101
Bradbrook, M. C., 98, 111
Brome, A., 90
Brown, W., 98
Browning, R. B., 123

Index